ELEVATOR
MAN

STORIES

JIM COLLETT

ELEVATOR MAN
STORIES

This Book Is Dedicated To My Dad

For information please contact: ElevatorGear.com, LLC, 4751 N. Olcott Avenue Harwood Heights, IL 60706 or Jim Collett, 601 Drake Ave # 2 Monterey, CA 93940

ISBN 1453692282
EAN13 9781453692288

ElevatorGear.com books are available for special promotions and premiums. For details contact Tom Sybert at ElevatorGear.com, LLC, 4751 N. Olcott Avenue, Harwood Heights, IL 60706 or contact Jim Collett, 601 Drake Ave # 2, Monterey, CA 93940

Editor: Patti Christy
Book Design: Tom Sybert

FIRST EDITION

FOREWORD

The idea for this book came from several places. My father, after retiring from the business, moved to Apple Valley, California. I spent many happy hours with him reminiscing about the old times and about the business we both shared. When I started with Haughton as a Junior Draftsman, Dad would hold school with me at the kitchen table five nights a week. After I left the office for the field there were many opportunities to work alongside him as his Helper. Several years after his passing, my mother suggested I write about my experiences and the people with whom I worked in the elevator business. I took her advice to heart.

I started with a weekly blog that sparked the interest of Tom Sybert, the host of "The Elevator Radio Show" podcast. Tom, for the last year, has encouraged me to keep going and finish this work. It would never have been possible to finish this book without the untiring help from my wife, Patti. She has painstakingly corrected my spelling, grammar and sentence structure to help me achieve a finished product.

Many thanks again to Mom, Patti and Tom.

My Father James Vance Collett

Local No. 18

March 1 1946

TEMPORARY WORKING CARD

issued to James V. Collett

for a period of One Month.

from March 1 19 46, to April 5 19 46

but no longer.

Issued by E. W. Tubbs

Business Representative

CONTENTS

Jim Collett & Bud – 1968

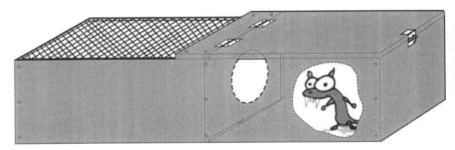

Mongoose Box – Tricks of the Trade - Chapter 4

CHAPTER ONE
Beginnings

My father, Vance, served in the Navy during WWII. He grew up in San Bernardino where he received his degree in electrical engineering. He was an avid "Amateur Radio Operator" (HAM). When WWII broke out, he enlisted in the United States Navy. With his qualifications from civilian life, the Navy sent him to Oklahoma A&M from where he was commissioned as an Ensign. He was then assigned to Treasure Island, California as an instructor in the use and repair of radar and radio equipment. By VJ Day, he'd been promoted to the rank of Lieutenant and transferred to the Great Lakes Naval Station in Chicago. He was put in command of the radio and radar training division.

When he returned to California, his brother, Nelson, was able to steer Dad in the right direction so he could hire on with Otis. Nelson was a longtime Otis employee. Starting as a Helper, he worked his way through the ranks to become a Service Manager in Los Angeles. Dad started as a typical "grunt" in the construction department for Otis in LA. With his electrical background, he was able to work his way up to Adjuster. He started out adjusting the smaller jobs like 10/20Us and hydro freights in way-out places. He traveled all over the Western United States. He moved on to adjusting Class A installations such as Autotronics and 80Us. He tired of traveling and being away from home so he asked Otis for a service job. Within two months he was back on the road adjusting elevators ... the job he loved!

As a kid I was forced to visit this old barber. While getting my hair cut, he asked me what my dad did for a living. I told him he was an elevator man and worked for Otis Elevator. "No kidding," he replied, "I worked for Otis for a few days until I was drilling a hole in a hoist way and a bridge plank came down the hatch and left a row of slivers in the back of my jacket and that's how I became a barber."

Dad's job didn't just consist of adjusting elevators. During the building boom in the Western United States, Otis dominated the elevator market. They did most of the installations in hospitals and office buildings in the distant and smaller cities. They had installed their standard 10/20U duplex all over Arizona, California and Alaska. There was a problem with these units that started showing up in these installations. The duplexing would lock up both cars. On the smaller, gearless installations there was a different problem. The cars would stall in leveling and sit and cook. He was able to troubleshoot this problem while catching a stalled car in the act. The compounding was so touchy that the car couldn't make it into the floor under certain conditions. He grabbed the driver and moved it in the direction of travel and "bingo," the car leveled in. Being out in the sticks, a car could soak for days. Because of these problems, building personnel would have to hike the stairs and mainline both elevators to get them running again. Yonkers came out with a fix that Dad started installing in LA. The fix was extremely time-consuming and required a great deal of material. After installing the Yonkers fix on several cars in LA, he came up with his own fix. His fix only required a half-hour per car and 10 feet of wire. Yonkers approved his fix and it was back on the road again.

Alaska and Arizona had many of these installations. After applying his fix in Tucson and Phoenix, he was off to Alaska. He traveled to Juno, Fairbanks, Ketchikan, Anchorage and other small cities. There were times he flew in a two-engine seaplane. He always said he missed Mom and me during his time up there, but we knew he loved every minute of it.

In the late 50s, Elevator Maintenance Company (EMCO) recruited Dad. Working for EMCO brought forth a wealth of experience due to the diversity of equipment they built, bought and installed. Haughton bought EMCO a couple of years later, and it wasn't long before Dad became "Chief Adjuster." He adjusted everything from the old damping motor series field control to regulator generators and then moved on to tach feedback systems with 1092IC Group Supervisory Systems.

You name it, if Haughton shipped it out the backdoor, Dad fixed it, adjusted it and turned it over to the customer. His work was cut out for him. Haughton was experiencing severe growing pains. They were moving from the way elevators had always been built to the beginnings of the way elevators are today. Nothing worked! Everything had to be fixed in the field from governors, safeties, motor control and supervisory systems. Dad fixed it all. He nursed every new product the Company came out with, made it work, made it reliable and made sure the service department could keep it running well.

Mom always seemed to worry just a little when Dad went off to work. As a little kid I didn't know what was bothering her until one day there was a knock on our door. It was summer and our living room was filled with kids playing games, eating watermelon and just generally messing around. The man at the door turned out to be Phil, a fellow elevator man and one of Dad's best friends.

Mom asked us to be quiet and not trash the house while she was gone. When asked what happened, she told us Dad was hurt and Phil was taking her to the hospital. The next time I saw my father, he was in a hospital, flat on his back and not happy. He had been working on a toe guard junction box at the bottom floor, lost his balance and fell into the hoist way. The fall was a short one but it did its damage. He was very lucky because he hit the pit floor missing all the pit equipment. He was in a hospital bed for the next month or so and then rested at home for two months.

We visited him every day and during those visits he must have felt I was old enough to appreciate the dangers of working on elevators. He started telling me about his near misses and the not-so-fortunate results of other accidents in which he was involved.

While adjusting a car and getting it up to speed, a Helper, working in an adjacent hoist way had ventured too far into the hoist way belonging to Dad's running car. The car hit him and knocked him down the hoist way. The Helper fell two floors, severely breaking his arm. All work stopped so this man could be helped. Dad suggested keeping the man still and not moving him. He told them all to keep him as comfortable as possible until medical help arrived. He was overruled by the Foreman who was an old timer and thought he knew it all. Well, he didn't. The Foreman tied the broken arm to the man's chest with #16 wire and had him climb up a ladder to the landing. Two minutes later help arrived. Due to the extensive damage to the arm, the move and the shoddy first aid, he lost his arm.

Dad was working at another large job in LA when a skip with four men aboard fell eight floors when the rigging for the three-to-three rope blocks failed. Three men rode it out but didn't survive the impact. The fourth man managed to grab a spreader beam during the descent and was able to hang on; unfortunately, he was hit by the rest of the rigging coming down the hatch and was also killed.

During those days accidents were commonplace with no safety skips, guardrails or harnesses. The companies tried putting guardrails on the skips, but found out we would just use them to gain the extra height to work rather than pulling the skips up by hand. Also, there were always things coming down the hoist ways. Guardrails just barred our emergency exit so the crews resisted the idea. I, personally, never worked off a skip equipped with safeties until about 1970. Once the idea caught on and the crews got used to them, they saved many lives.

Dad went on to tell of a freak accident that happened on an out-of-town job. The crews were working four/tens in order to bail on Thursday so they could spend three days at home. It just so happened that after normal working hours, a full roll of carpet came down the hoist way and landed directly on top of one of the Mechanic's feet. The roll crushed his foot along with the steel toe that was supposed to protect it. The man never worked again and to make matters worse, the accident happened after contractual working hours, so he had a tough time getting his benefits.

Dad also told of a very unusual work assignment the Company gave him. A Service Mechanic had his hand in the wrong place while wiping down a machine. The driver sucked in the rag along with his hand and severed it at the wrist. The Mechanic had the presence of mind to apply a tourniquet and make it to the top floor lobby and ask the, understandably freaked out, receptionist to summon help. The severed hand had fallen through the cable block out and was resting on the car top. Dad rescued it and took it to the hospital. It was the 60s and there was no chance of it being re-attached.

The Company dispatched him to a Victorville cement plant to find the cause of death of an inside maintenance man who had been killed while working on one of the plant's elevators. The man had been crushed in the pit while he and another maintenance man were attempting to repair the elevator. Dad discovered the limit switches were not explosion-proof and concrete dust had filled them up to the point where the finger contacts couldn't open. This was a very sad story for the man's family and equally distressing for the other man who was running the elevator at the time.

He was involved in and investigated another fatality in Hawaii. Even in his later years he couldn't get this accident out of his mind.

A 200 pound man was in a disabled elevator. The building maintenance man opened the hoist way doors with a lunar key. The car was around 24 inches below the top of the entrance. The maintenance man, who was a little guy, got a ladder and entered the car. He then assisted the man down the ladder. While climbing out of the car it leveled up to the next landing, pinning the man at his midsection between the car and hoist way sill at the next floor. The man died shortly thereafter. The Fire Department arrived and suggested cutting the platform around the body to recover it. The elevator man who had arrived within minutes of the accident suggested tying a rope under the man's arms and running the car down on inspection. They decided that was the best approach and went ahead and the body ended up on the car. Dad found that the building had short floors and the elevator had a very long leveling zone. The weight of the 200 pound man stretched the ropes enough to keep the up-level switch off the next floor's leveling vane. After the man exited the car and the maintenance man stepped onto the ladder, the ropes outstretched to the point where the up-leveling switch engaged the vane and the car was able to level up to the next floor. Dad made the necessary controller changes to this non-Haughton equipment to prevent another accident.

On a much lighter note, he told me about the time he was working alone in a machine room of an occupied building. An exposed exciter shaft managed to grab his pant leg thus ripping them off his body. I can't seem to remember how he got out of that one.

The end of Dad's career was not pretty. His eyesight was beginning to fail. Being the proud, stubborn man he was, he refused to take a service route when offered by the Company. The Company didn't make a serious effort to utilize his wealth of talent. There is an old saying, "What Have You Done for Me Today." Never mind the years of dedicated service, problem-solving and loyalty. I don't want to start this story on a negative note. My father did retire in 1977, built his dream home in the desert and lived there until he passed in 1993.

My father's greatest attribute was teaching. While in the Navy his students must have saved many lives by detecting the enemy before he arrived. He not only taught union school, but he taught his Helpers well. Most of his Helpers went on to become Adjusters, Route men, Service Managers, Superintendents and even successful elevator company owners. He always took the time to answer questions and made sure they were understood.

CHAPTER TWO
One Giant Step

In 1961 I got a job as a junior draftsman at Haughton Elevator Company located at 1316 Glendale Blvd in Los Angeles. My dad was an Adjuster for the Company and was able to get me through the front door. I considered myself lucky. Haughton had been in business for almost 100 years and was a subsidiary of Toledo Scale. They were headquartered in the Midwest and they were a longtime manufacturer of large AC freights for industry in the Rust Belt. In the 1950s they moved into the passenger end of the elevator business. Looking forward to expanding to the West Coast, in 1957 they purchased EMCO. EMCO installed, serviced, modernized and repaired elevator equipment up and down the West Coast. They didn't only do elevator work; they installed ammunition lifts on ships, man-lifts at missile sites, large lifts on ships and so on. They took on any type of vertical transportation job. The Glendale Boulevard facility had administrative offices, an engineering department, a parts warehouse and a cab shop on one side of the street. They had a fabrication shop along with a panel shop (controllers) on the other side of the street. They didn't just manufacture their equipment; they purchased and installed equipment from companies like Warsaw, Elevator Supply, GE and GAL to name a few. Monte, the owner, had come to EMCO from Llewellyn Iron Works when EMCO was still a small company. He became the owner and managed to turn EMCO into one of the largest independent elevator companies in Los Angeles by recruiting the best people in the business ... a prime example was my Uncle Nelson. Nelson was the Western-area Service Manager for Otis. Monte hired him, doubled his salary and gave him a blue Cadillac for a Company car. Another talent was my father, an Adjuster for Otis. Monte paid him 15% over scale and also provided a Company car. The bottom line was, he took great care of his people. If an employee, union or nonunion, came upon hard times, Monte would help him out with a loan. There were always Thanksgiving turkeys and hams. His field people never lacked for tools. He employed a fulltime tool man to track, maintain and issue tools. You name it and the tool man had it.

As stated earlier, Monte bought the best people and took good care of them as well. He kept a tight rein on his business by keeping track of everything that went on in the Glendale Boulevard office. He had an audio surveillance system installed through the office, bathrooms excluded. It was all connected to his small office perched on top of the building which was only accessible by a home lift. That way he could sit in his office and monitor every conversation that took place in his domain.

After the Haughton acquisition, there were a lot of oddball jobs to clean up and from that point forward, for the most part, only Haughton equipment would be installed with one exception, the West Coast Hydro which was still being manufactured right on Glendale Boulevard and ...

THIS IS WHERE MY STORY BEGINS ...!

On the first day at Haughton, I reported to Frank, the Chief Engineer. Frank, a former Llewellyn employee, was an older man who had been in the elevator business for many years. Frank and Monte's former employer, Llewellyn, had a long history in Southern California.

After the fire and earthquake in San Francisco (1906) Llewellyn installed the first elevator constructed in a building subsequent to that disaster. They also supervised the installation of elevators in most of the large buildings in Los Angeles, including the Alexandria Hotel and the Los Angeles Athletic Club. It was a great company and way ahead of its time. They made some of the finest car switch elevators. All were equipped with Randall pneumatic doors and a cable-operated master door lock.

Some had collapsible car gates and some had no car entrance protection. Their elevators were even equipped with car top inspection.

Llewellyn, along with Baker Iron Works, had a large presence in Los Angeles. Llewellyn competed with Otis on Class "A" gearless installations. Llewellyn built beautiful equipment. They bought their gearless hoist motors and generators from Westinghouse Electric and built everything else in their factory. As the story goes, they ran into financial difficulties and were also on the hook to Westinghouse Electric for big bucks. At that time Westinghouse wanted to get into the elevator business so a deal was brokered, and they bought out Llewellyn. The rest is history.

As mentioned earlier, Baker Iron Works manufactured oil-boring tools and rigs, and constructed both passenger and freight elevators in all varieties, e.g., hydraulic steam or hand. It was claimed by the newspaper that Baker had installed nearly all the first class passenger elevators in Southern California. After the turn of the century, Baker specialized in steel fabrication and elevator construction. Over the next 30 years, they did the steel work for elevators and for the first skyscraper in Los Angeles, the twelve-story Union Trust Building. They also did the steel work for the Public Service Building, the Queen of Angels Hospital, the YWCA Hotel, the United Artists building, the California Petroleum

Building, UCLA in Westwood and The Masonic Temple in Glendale.

I found Frank to be a great guy to work for and one hell of an elevator engineer.

Next in command was another great elevator man, Alex. Alex was a longtime EMCO employee who had started in 1946 with Beckwith and was recruited by Monte in 1952. Beckwith was a smaller company that specialized in hydraulic elevators of all types. They installed water hydraulic elevators with central pressurized systems. The central reservoir was pressurized by steam-driven compressors and later by electric compressors. This single pressurized reservoir would supply water pressure to several elevators. Alex knew the business better than any man I have or ever will meet, not to mention, he was a "Prince of a Guy."

My immediate boss was Gordon, another former Beckwith employee. Gordon was excellent at what he did and he was also a great guy. Gordon stayed in the business for many years to follow. He formed his own company and the last I heard, he had successfully retired and was enjoying life.

Then there was Fran, the First Sergeant of the engineering department. She handled just about everything from ordering blueprints to breaking up squabbles among the draftsmen.

While working with Gordon, my job included ordering the electrical equipment from our shop and warehouse and then putting together the electrical portion of the job folder. The job folder included wiring diagrams, drawings for the hoist way electrical equipment including fixtures for the Haughton West Coast Hydro. I also drew up wiring diagrams for non-standard features such as rear openings, duplex operation, hoist way access, attendant operation and heavy duty operators.

Gordon and I were in the process of standardizing the West Coast Hydro by adding more options to the standard wiring diagrams. We were also working on modularizing the controllers. For instance, if the elevator required a rear opening, the wireman in the panel shop could pull a prewired module off the shelf, install it in the controller and then make the interconnections from a wiring table. I have to say this really worked out. We also made changes to existing elevator wiring diagrams that showed changes to correct operational problems or new features.

Haughton installed hundreds of West Coast Hydro's. There were times I was processing five new elevators a week. These were great little elevators. They were very well built and used first class components. There are hundreds of them still running today. Alex was behind all this and his basic design went on to be incorporated into Haughton's newer midrise traction elevators. The Stepping Switch Modular, early Haughton traction elevators used mostly

23

208 VAC for all logic functions, 24 VAC for signals and 120 VAC for lanterns. This was a throwback from the exciter days. With better rectifiers, he could use 110 VDC for everything except for the motor control. On midrise jobs, he replaced the old floor-mounted selectors with a stepping switch just 100th their size.

I became friends with the Construction Super, Frank. He was the Haughton LA Office Construction Superintendent. He was a big, tall guy and former Construction Mechanic/Foreman with a great sense of humor and absolutely no sense of fashion. Frank always looked like an unmade bed. His only brown suit he wore was so stiff and unkempt it probably beat him home at night to find its place standing in the corner of his bedroom. His "tie," and I say "tie," because he only had one, had enough old dried food on it that when scraped off, would probably feed a family of 12 for a month.

He was a great boss though, so his men loved him and would work their tails off for him. Frank worked for Hugh, the Construction Manager. Hugh was also a big guy who ran a tight ship.

Hugh was a veteran of The Battle of the North Atlantic. He flew a PBY4-1 which was the Navy version of the B24 Liberator. His PBY4-1 provided air cover for the convoys that were England's lifeline. It's hard to imagine the anti-submarine patrols above an endless unforgiving grey sea, all the while depending on skill and the airplane you were flying to keep you and your crew from an almost certain fate in the freezing waters below. He had to contend with eleven-hour flying times, horrible weather and emergency landings in places like Greenland. The Liberator's long range allowed it to fly out of the Canadian Maritimes or Scotland to protect the brave Merchant Mariners who were risking their lives in the ships below. Hugh was also checked out in Vought F4F Corsairs which he loved to fly. His only complaint was, while landing, he couldn't see forward due to the huge radial engine that could push this War Bird to 400 plus miles per hour. By the end of the War, he was flying PBY Catalina's again on submarine patrols. Hugh, along with many others, brought WWII to an end with his dedication to duty, skill and not to mention, "Just Plain Guts."

Sometimes Hugh ran the construction department a little too tight. Frank was a very effective buffer between Hugh, the Construction Manager and the field personnel.

Hughes right-hand-man was Al, a great little guy and longtime EMCO employee. Al took care of payroll and basically kept the whole deal running. Frank was very entertaining and funnier than hell. In today's world his pranks and wise cracks involving the female employees in the office would violate all the sexual harassment laws on the books. And maybe a few that hadn't even been thought of yet.

After about a year in the office and me dropping subtle hints to Frank, he agreed to give me a chance as a 50% Construction Helper. The 50% pay rate was new and had only been in effect for a few months. Prior to that time a starting Helper earned 70% of what a journeyman Mechanic earned. At that time, the hourly rate for a 50 per center was about $8 per hour. I stayed in the office for two more weeks, until embarking on the greatest adventure of my life.

CHAPTER THREE
Out to the Field

Before starting work in the field, I had to visit the local union office to pick up my work permit.

The local 18 office was just off Wilshire Boulevard near McArthur Park in LA. When I got there, I was greeted by a woman who had her speedometer rolled back about 100,000 miles. I also noticed this heavyset guy sitting behind a desk in the back office. I later learned the lady in front was Eve and the guy in the back was John, our Business Manager. I introduced myself and told them I needed a temporary working card. Suddenly, there was a chill in the air and the two became as cold as ice. I found out later this chilly reception was due to the ongoing feud between my father and John. Eve threw me some paperwork to fill out which was the basic information request: name, age, address and the basics. After completing the form she handed me five sheets of paper that turned out to be a test. Then she pointed to a side office and told me I could go in there and complete the test.

All this activity must have alerted John, and he started to take some interest in my test taking. He snuffed out his Camel in an overflowing ashtray and in a gruff voice he said, "Can he drive a sixteen-penny straight?" Eve laughed and took a long drag on a Pall Mall and said, "I don't know, John." Later it became apparent the only nails John knew about were the nails he was driving into his own coffin (coffin nails).

The written test was pretty basic with questions like; Can you find your ass with both hands? ... Do you know shit from Shinola? Do you have to show up on time?   That one was multiple choice! I passed the test with flying colors and left the building with my brand, spanking new "Temporary Working Permit" just like the one Dad had in 1946.

On my very first day I reported to the Haughton shop dressed in my new J.C. Penny's work shirt, Levi 501s and my high-top Red Wing steel-toed work boots. It felt just like the first day of school. I was told to bring a screwdriver, channel locks, a notebook, a ruler, a pencil and a pocket knife. Frank took one look at me and snickered, "Ain't He Purrrt-y."

All along the question in my head was ... where would my first work assignment be? As I held my breath, he told me to go to the Federal Office Building (FOB) in Downtown Los Angeles. Oh no, not the Federal Building!!! FOB was a big job with sixteen gearless passenger cars, two geared service cars, one hydro and a couple of escalators. The whole shebang was all under one roof in a big rectangular box at Los Angeles & Temple Streets. Also, FOB just happened to be the "Devil's Island" of Haughton's current jobs. To make matters worse, the Foreman was the Devil himself ... "Bud."

I drove my '58 Ford Fairlane 500 down the Hollywood Freeway to the Temple Street exit, parked on the street about five blocks from the job, gathered up my stuff, hiked on in and started looking for Bud. I'd never been on a big job before, and it was downright SCARY. Here were all these mean-looking hardhats. They were yelling at each other and even taking a crap on toilets right out in the open, close enough to whisper in each others' ear.

Then there were the "big-ass" holes in the floor that went into some dark unknown abyss. Power cords were all over the floor. It was dark and the only lighting came from two wires strung everywhere with light bulbs attached via a plastic device called a Redhead. To top it off, there was the ear-shattering noise that came from everywhere.

I found Bud, introduced myself to the "Alleged Tyrant" who responded with a few primeval undistinguishable grunts. Rather than the elevator Superman I expected, here stood a short, stocky guy wearing a J.C. Penny's Towncraft navy blue tee-shirt with a

Marlboro hard pack in the pocket. This guy had the shortest, thickest fingers I'd ever seen. And to make matters worse, he chewed his nails, and they looked like those old "MOON" wheel covers cut in half. Later I found out, they were the source of his nickname, Stumpy.

The Federal Office Building was eight stories tall but the equivalent to a 12 to 15 story building due to 20 foot floor heights. There was no personnel hoist so our only way up and down was the stairs or our skips. The skips were platforms constructed of plywood and 2x4s that were built to fit between the elevator guiderails. They were propelled up the hoist way by a large geared 220 volt motor at the bottom landing secured with a 4x4 wedged into the ceiling. On the end of the motor was a capstan (cathead). The 3x3 rope blocks (3 to 3s) using manila rope, were suspended from the overhead of the hoist way and attached to the center of the skip. To travel up, the free line from the upper rope block was wrapped around the cathead and turned on by a guy at the bottom landing using a footswitch. If the cathead was not available we pulled the skips up by hand. Traveling down was a different deal as seen later in my story.

My first ride on this 7x8 foot piece of plywood was with four other guys whose average weight had to be 240 lbs. Along with all this muscle and beer belly, there were 100 pounds of tools and mysterious elevator stuff. We got on the skip in the basement.

I crowded close to the center to avoid certain death by falling off the edge into the empty space which surrounded us on all sides. One of the guys hit the steel rail two times with a large hammer (single-jack). The skip started up with a jerk and after traveling up four floors, the single-jack struck one time again and we stopped. Bud growled, "This is us." We stepped off the skip onto a lobby that had four open hoist ways on each side. There were about 5 rectangular iron, rusty things called counterweight fillers spread all over the unfinished lobby floor. Bud informed me my job would be to pick up one of these 150 pounds of iron, carry it across the lobby and place it on a waiting skip parked waist high. After I loaded six of these monsters, I banged on the rail twice and like magic the weights and skip disappeared up the hoist way. After three hours of this I could see my hemorrhoids peeking out of the bottom of my pant leg. I was already beat and it wasn't even lunchtime yet.

Just as the skip mysteriously disappeared three hours ago, it suddenly reappeared in the dark hoist way like something right out of a Stephen King movie. On board were the same four behemoths as before. Bud said, "Get on, time for lunch." The trip down was different from the trip up. To begin with, there was no room at the center this time and believe me, you didn't want to grab onto one of the other guys. The first day on the job was not the time for lasting impressions. One of the guys had wrapped a length of rope around the rope falls four times and was holding each end. This was our descent velocity control. The less he pulled the ends, the faster we went. The harder he pulled, the slower we went. Pulling even harder caused us to stop. "Ok," he said ... and down we went ... and fast. My first thought was, "I'm going to die" but the other guys were looking at me and grinning ... It must be okay, I guess.

The elevator business is a hazardous business. I have and will continue to tell our humorous, everyday stories but due to the nature of the business, I must include the personal tragedies as well.

The ropes were smoking as we traveled down the hoist way at Mach 10. A new guy, Roy, panicked and grabbed the whizzing ropes with both hands. With five ropes traveling faster than we were and moving in opposite directions to boot, it was the fast thinking of the guy with the rope controlling our speed to stop the skip before any serious damage was done to Roy's hands.

Haughton had recently hired five new 50 per centers. These new guys, like me, were all about 20 years of age except for Roy. He had at least 10 to 15 years on the rest of us and was no ball of fire but the guy tried as hard as he could. Bud treated this poor guy like a galley slave and was on his ass for anything and everything. Roy was also accident-prone and had already emptied out two of our first aid kits and was always covered with band aids. Earlier in the job Roy had incorrectly grabbed a rail on the end while it was being hoisted into the hoist way. He had his hands underneath the end when the center of the rail wedged in the top of the entrance. Roy's hands were now wedged between the sharp end of the rail and the unfinished raked concrete floor. The rail kept moving, peeling his knuckles off. Roy's safety record on the job wasn't the greatest, but we do know he must have had a stellar safety record on the freeway. More than once he was spotted driving to and from the job in his green and white Nash Metropolitan wearing his hardhat at a rakish tilt. We all felt he should be in another line of work. As it turns out, he had a close relative who was an elevator inspector.

Later in the job, the shop asked for a crew to do a small job in Bakersfield, so Bud gleefully sent Roy and a Mechanic, Carl, to do the job. Carl weighed in at around 300 hundred pounds and could only sit and wire controllers. We'd all get a kick out of him when he'd grab his leather belt with both hands and loop it up over his belly just like a lineman climbing a telephone pole.

Roy somehow made Mechanic as a Serviceman years later at an independent elevator company in LA. In the 80s he was answering an overtime call and, while working on the broken elevator, made a serious mistake which cost him his life.

As the story goes, he answered a call on a duplex. He entered the pit of the running car without turning it off and then reached in between the counter weight rails of the running elevator to work on the adjacent car. The weights came down and severed his arm. He lay in the pit and bled to death long before a family member called the Company and reported him missing. They finally dispatched another Mechanic to check on Roy; it was way too late.

Lunch was usually a quick dash to the "Gut Wagon" to grab a beef and potato "Ramona" burrito, which was handmade in the City of Industry. If you missed out on the first choice you had to settle for a burrito created, God only knows where. These gut bombs were unlabeled, undated, damn near inedible and filled with an unknown magic substance known only as "textured vegetable protein." The mysterious crud wrapped inside a tortilla did have a good side; its magical properties could cure the worst hangover.

Our shack was a large room in the basement where we ate lunch and stored our material and tools. Inside there was a well-defined class structure. The Mechanics and the 70% Helpers were grouped in one area. The 50% Helpers sat in another group. The only time the line could be crossed is if a younger 50 per center had a graphic sex story. The older Mechanics would listen with keen interest and sometimes drool or even drift into a memory-induced stupor. They would always tease us about our love lives and demand to hear the most vivid details. After awhile we 50 per centers started getting together over beers and made up stories "Hustler Magazine" wouldn't even print. This made-up material was then fed to the older Mechanics a little at a time. As the stories grew more incredible the closer we got to the inner circle.

As a 50% Helper on a large job you were the lowest of the low. You normally didn't work with a specific Mechanic. You were more like a get it, lift it, move it, store it, push it, unpack it, open it and clean it but never install it. You spoke only when spoken to, stayed busy and kept your mouth shut. And God help you if you didn't have your channel locks, screwdriver, ruler, pencil and notepad and pocket knife. If a Mechanic told you to drop your pants at 5th and Grand in Downtown LA … you DID it!

In the 60s, the elevator trade could be compared to the three books of Dante's Divine Comedy. The first book, "Inferno" was the 50 per centers. The second book, "Purgatory" was the 70 per centers and finally, "Paradise" was the Mechanics and Foremen.

Bud laid out Roy's and my next assignment. The basement of FOB was full of hoist way doors for the two service cars which were two-speed center open. That meant four doors per car and eight doors per landing, all of them over 100 pounds each. Bud grunted, "Unpack and carry them up the stairs, distribute them at each landing without scratching so the two crews working in the hoist way can hang them, got the picture studs?" We got the picture and carried doors up the stairs for two days. The only redeeming part of this endeavor was that the crews had started hanging doors at the top landing, so our trip got shorter as they progressed down the hoist way. I slept very well that night.

I had a chance to work with several different Mechanics while in and out of FOB. One in particular was Larry. He was a Bull Mechanic who was the terror of all Helpers. He was a big guy with a barrel chest, deep, loud voice and close-cropped hair. He was also a hell-raiser who could hold his own with just about anybody. It was a very bad idea to cross Larry. When pissed, he could be like a rattlesnake with a case of hives. His dress for work was a little different than the rest of us; it consisted of a short-sleeve sport shirt, grey Levies and cowboy boots, not exactly a poster child for OSHA.

This guy was a Helper's nightmare. He could pick up two counter weight rails, one in each hand and carry them a long distance, over all types of terrain, in order to get them to the hoist way, and that's pushing over 200 pounds. The major rub here is somebody had to be on the other end. That somebody was his Helper, big or small. He went through Helpers like Imelda Marcos went through shoes. Today he might be known as, "The Helper Cookie Monster."

He usually started traction jobs by installing the rails and pit equipment, hoisting the generators, machines and controllers and then pulling off. Thus he was called a Bull Mechanic. That reference really pissed him off. He worked hard, drank hard and expected his Helper to do likewise.

When we worked together at FOB we spent our time re-rigging skips and untangling the kinks in the manila rope in the pit so the skips could travel up and down without stopping. The kinks and tangles in the rope were known as "Assholes" in elevator talk. We used terms such as "Down the Road" (fired, laid off or sent to the shop), "Grunt" (Helper), "Pusher" (Foreman), "Can You do it Boy?" (Get with it) and "My Mother's Slow, But She's 80 Years Old" (hurry up). All these terms and some others I can't recall were adopted by elevator constructors from high linemen. By the way, the comeback to "Can You Do it Boy?" was, "With a Slop Jar Full of N**s And a Nine-Inch C**k ..."And You Call Me Boy?"

I worked with Larry for a few months, and we got along just fine. Sorry to say, some years later I heard he had moved to Denver, taken a job as a route Mechanic, cleaned up his act and remarried. While on a service call, he picked the door lock and, while stepping on the car top, tripped and fell into the hoist way on the front of the elevator. The hoist way doors closed behind him, the car started up and crushed him to death.

We had the last eight passenger cars to rope and that would do it for the roping for all sixteen cars.

Roping the elevators was a group effort. We'd start by shackling the ends of the one-half inch steel rope by feeding the rope through the shackle and turning back the strands to form a rosette. The ropes were lubricated in the factory and the individual strands on the ends were like needles. The "Blood Pool" was setup and the "First to Bleed" would be buying the first "Round" later that afternoon. The Babbitt was heated until melted and poured into the socket of the shackle. It was heated in an iron pot with a propane tank below. The right temperature was reached when a sliver of wood would just start to burn when dipped into the pot. Some of the older Mechanics took great pleasure in shocking the 50 per centers ... you'd hear, "That's not the way to check it"... and the Mechanic would stick his finger into to the molten Babbitt for a couple of seconds without getting burned. The new guys couldn't believe it, freaked out and didn't know whether to head for the first aid kit or put a call into the closest burn center. This was an old trick they played on the new guys. After handling the wire rope with its factory lube, their hands and fingers had excellent insulation against the heat thus avoiding being burned.

Our Babbitt pot served another very important function; it cut down sick days for the guys who had to buy their lunch off the "Gut Wagon." During lunch we would fire it up and heat the sandwiches and burritos they purchased. Heating this jobsite cuisine to a temperature just short of combustion would kill Beriberi, E-Coli, Dysentery and all the creeping crud that had setup housekeeping in these ptomaine coaches-on-wheels.

"Nick the Cable Man" was Haughton's go-to cable guy and fit the picture perfectly, with rolled up sleeves, butch haircut and big muscled arms with tattoos to match. He came by one day to pick up some Babbitt and gave us a short demonstration of his skills. He could turn a rosette just using his bare fingers and to show off he crimped it back with his teeth.

We started roping by setting up a spool of rope on a cable roller at the top landing where the skip was also parked. The counterweight frame was tied off at the proper height which was accessible from the skip. The shackled end was attached to a length of manila rope dropped down from the machine room on the counter weight side. The guy in the machine room pulled the shackled end of the rope up into the machine room, fed it over the hoist motor and dropped it down to a man waiting on the skip below. He fed it down the hoist way through one of two holes cut out in the skip. A guy on a ladder on the elevator platform fed it around the car sheave and attached it to a rope that was fed through a snatch block attached in the overhead. We pulled the shackled cable back up the hoist way and attached it to the dead end hitch in the overhead. The cable was then pulled off the spool, passed to the guy on the skip who fed it around the counterweight sheave and passed it up to the guy in the dead end hitch space where he marked it and passed it back down to be shackled up. The shackled rope was passed up the dead end hitch where a guy in the dead end space put the nuts on the shackle.

A lot going on here, it took four guys but we had a running service car. A running elevator made it a lot easier to get from the top landing to the bottom landing to feed cable around the sheave and send it back up the hoist way. We did this six times per elevator.

One day a semi arrived with the hoist way doors for the sixteen passenger elevators. When opened up, the trailer revealed cardboard boxed doors stacked from floor to ceiling and end to end. That worked out to be over two hundred boxes at one hundred pounds each. That truck just brought us 20,000 pounds of doors and only doors.

The whole crew unloaded them all day and from that point on it was up to us grunts to unpack and distribute 32 doors per floor. This time we didn't have to carry doors up the stairs. Thanks to the Adjusters, we had running platforms for transportation.

We started hanging hoist way doors, installing electrical piping, assembling machine room gutter, and installing fixture boxes. Bud found out I could read wiring diagrams. I teamed up with Dale and started pulling wire. Dale, also a 50 per center, was this big, tall, red-headed kid from Seattle and also the Construction Manager's cousin. He took a whole lot of flak over that relationship but just smiled and said, "You bet, and I'm cleaning out his garage this weekend." We became great friends and spent our time drinking beer and visiting car shows.

He had just bought one of the first Pontiac GTOs. We had about a week off due to a walk-off over downtown parking. So we headed for Seattle to see the country and party with his friends while consuming mass quantities of Union-Made Olympia Beer. The GTO was very fast, I think some of the local towns on Route 99 could have installed their first street lights with the revenue collected from the speeding tickets we collected while zooming through their little Podunk towns.

Later in Dale's career he went back to Seattle and hired on with Sound Elevator and became one of their top hands. Sound was one of the Pacific Northwest's largest independents ... family owned and operated with a stellar reputation to boot. Most Mechanics would have given their left nut, or at least part of it, to work for them. Sound went the way of most good companies and sold out to

Thyssen. The last I heard, Dale made it to retirement and is restoring classic airplanes.

We had Mechanics and Helpers coming and going all the time. The Mechanics had two questions when they hit the job ... "Where can I unload my tools and where can I park?" The job was well enough along so parking wasn't a problem.

The General Contractor had finished two parking levels and allowed the trades to use them. The garages had the same footprint as the building, which made them huge. Around the perimeter was a newly installed heavy duty guardrail at bumper height. We'd help the new arrival unload his stuff and show him where to park. We'd inform him it was better to back in because quitting time was a zoo. Backing out would be almost impossible because of the exiting traffic. After getting the new guy settled, a decision had to be made. Do we get the kit? The kit was stashed in a gang box in the parking garage, and it consisted of a six and one-half inch steel choker and a shackle. A short conference was held out of sight of the newcomer. A "yes" meant one of us would get the kit and tightly secure the newcomer's bumper to the steel guard rail using the choker and shackle. We didn't want any slack in the connection so as not to damage bumper or guardrail. The minutes seemed to crawl by until quitting time, but it was well worth the wait. Trying not to be too obvious, we stationed ourselves in a spot which provided the view of the impending prank. After busting your tail for Bud all day, the only thought in your head was, "getting the hell out of there and the first cold one." The new guy would get into his tethered vehicle, fire it up and start heading for home.

Ever been to a drag race and seen the burn off? Well, we spectators had it all and didn't even have to buy a ticket. The best part was it took about three tries before the driver got it. And, best yet was, every time he tried to launch his car/truck and failed, he would give it even more gas and try again. After the smoke cleared and the red-faced driver got out of his vehicle, he was welcomed with cheers and applause, which was the complement of the 20 or so guys who were watching the spectacle from their hiding places in the nooks and crannies of the garage.

All this coming and going required a method of identifying personal hand tools, so the Mechanics painted their tools different colors. Some examples I remember were: Bud (Stumpy) yellow, John (Dirty John) blue, George (Catfish) black, Kelly (TJ) green/orange and so on. While working, tools were traded back and forth to get the job done.

When leaving a large job with several crews working together, there was always a departing ritual. The guy leaving would dump his hand tray on the floor so the other guys could find their tools. This not only redistributed the hand tools, but it also got rid of all the dirt and assorted hardware that had accumulated in the bottom of the hand tray. Needless to say, the hand tray became a much lighter load for the Helper to carry.

Back then there was no multi cable so before the wiring began the Adjusters got together with the wiring diagrams and made out 8x11 inch dope sheets that assigned the actual factory terminals with the easy code tags that we put on the wire. Dale and I setup four to six spools of wire with a length of pipe sitting on two sawhorses. We then pulled the wire down the hallway to the proper length. The wires back at the spools were tagged with the same number that was on the other end. We cut the wire at the spool end and started all over again with the next numbers. The run sometimes contained over 100 wires. We taped the wires together and wound the bundle on a larger spool so it could be dropped down the hoist way, pulled between machine room panels and onto the car itself. The easy codes came in colors, so we used different colors to identify different runs. White was used for the car only. Other colors were used for runs such as: controller to controller, selector to controller, dispatch to controller and signal panel to controller and so on.

In the machine room, along with the machines, generators, controllers and selectors, there were signal panels (group service), auxiliary panels (used when the controller ran out of room for relays) and a throw-over panel (for emergency power). They were all interconnected with the bundles of wire pulled earlier.

y

44

Other bundles were fed down the hoist way to the halfway junction box from the controller. From that point on, traveling cables were connected from the halfway junction box to the junction box on the car.

Traveling cables were color coded rather than numbered. The color coding started with the basic colors; stripes or traces were added to identify additional wires. Hoist way wiring was usually pulled as individual wires with the commons soldered in the gutter. We then started the actual wiring. We'd cut and strip, replace the easy code, crimp on a T&B ring terminal and attach it to a labeled #8 stud. This could go on for days.

It can get a little dicey when several cars are involved. I was working a three-car mod in LA when, after hooking up the car junction box and controller, a strange thing happened at startup.

In those days, we hooked up a temp station to run the car for construction. The temp station came with a long cord and was mounted on a piece of 10x16 inch plywood. This was a tool that came from the shop and, like all Haughton tools, was painted blue and yellow. It had industrial buttons and switches that came from Allen Bradley. It had an up, down, safe, stop and MG switch. Usually an Adjuster would get the cars running on temporary by hooking up a temp station to the controller. He setup the compounding to keep the car from going into orbit, checked that it traveled in both directions at a safe speed and then left. It was up to us to rewire the temp station to the car junction box so we could run the car from the platform. On the first, second, third and fourth try the temp station buttons wouldn't move the car. It looked like we had a little wiring problem and boy, did we! The fog cleared when one of the other trades came by with a news flash … "You know that last car over there is moving all by itself?" I said, "What do you mean?" He replied, "Not the one you're working on … that one over there." It wasn't that hard to figure out what went wrong.

When sitting on your butt, wiring in the machine room, you always watch out of the corner of your eye for "Bud" standing more or less just out of sight. I swear he always wore a sweatshirt that matched the surroundings. Bare steel was rust colored, bare steel with fireproofing was cream colored and so on. Bud was a master at camouflage. We never really did figure out whether he planned it or it was simply a coincidence.

To keep track of us he installed an intercom system, so he could communicate with the machine room. When the intercom was hooked up for the first time we didn't know he could listen in. One of the Mechanics, while unaware Bud was listening said, "Why don't we put the damn thing outside so he can talk to the sea gulls." In truth, I must admit, it was pretty handy since the shack was eight floors away.

Bud and I started to get along. He was okay when not in front of the rest of the crew. I became his Helper, which was a good job to have. He would lay out my work and tell or show me how to do it. He usually took off to pursue his "Pusher" duties. When I ran out of work it was time to pick up a broom. I learned a lot from Bud because he always took time to make sure I "Got the Picture, Stud?" The most important lesson was safety. Bud was tough as hell to work for. That became apparent during the 101-day strike when some of the Mechanics went to work as longshoremen. The real Longshoremen said, "Hey, you guys really work hard as hell." "Yeah right, you don't know who we have to work for," the Mechanics answered. Mechanics and Helpers always bitched and moaned but sometimes forgot, "Bud's jobs were safe jobs." He always made sure our rigging, roping and awareness was first class. Speaking of that, we did most of our hoisting using manila rope. Tying the knot correctly not only meant you kept your job; more importantly, it meant someone else kept his life.

The commonly used knots were: Bowline, used for most hoisting when using a single whip, usually attached to a clevis or shackle when running rails, and Square Knot, used when joining two lengths of line together. The manila rope was sometimes double-wrapped around beams with a snatch block or single block attached to the loop for lighter hoisting, such as rails. We also double wrapped it around a rail and bracket to secure a skip while re-rigging when removing the three-to-three rope blocks. A Becket was used to attach the dead end of a line to the ring on the upper three-to-three rope block. A painter's hitch was used on the live end of three-to-three rigging to secure a skip.

Bud and I actually became good friends over the years and even caught a few fish together. Later he fished with me on my own commercial fishing boat, The Vance III.

CHAPTER FOUR
The Tricks of the Trade

Elevator guys are a pretty clever bunch with good memories. I can't prove an elevator man invented this device but because of them, this time-honored prank keeps re-surfacing and keeps on "pranking" about every five years.

Construction is relatively simple:

Build a wooden box approximately twelve inches wide, twenty-four inches long and six inches deep.

Cover the bottom with a solid piece of plywood or hardboard.

Cover half of the top with chicken wire or hardware cloth.

Fit a piece of one-half inch plywood that has a centered four-inch-round hole in the center of the box.

Attach a one inch by two inch cross brace across the middle.

Attach the door which is an eleven by twelve inch piece of one-half inch plywood to the one-half inch by two inch cross brace using two spring loaded hinges.

Attach a hook to the inside of the door on the opening side.

Now you have a Mongoose Box ...

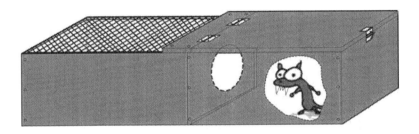

The spring loaded hinges must open the door outward. Secure the spring loaded door to the box with a finger activated latch; finally, find an old coonskin cap.

Pre-operation is relatively simple as well. Secure the coonskin cap to the hook on the door. While closing the door, feed the tail into the screened section through the hole in the center of the box. While closing and latching the door, tip the box up on the screened end so the cap's tail hangs vertically then set the box down and wait ...

Normally, there is no need to pitch the prank. Curiosity will bring your victims to you. "What do you have in there?" "It's a Mongoose," is your answer. "Does it bite?" Your next answer, "You bet, so be careful." You may have to pick up the pace at this point by saying, "Maybe I can get him to come out so you can see him." "Yeah, okay," the pigeon will answer. Now here comes the finesse. While tilting the box forward toward your victim say, "Come on out so we can see you, aw come on." The idea here is to get your victim as close as possible to the screened section of the box. When satisfied with the proximity of your victim, release the latch on the door, exclaiming, "Oh my God!" He's loose," just as the coonskin cap brushes the victim's face.

Enjoy . . .

CHAPTER FIVE
Other People, Other Mechanics

The Katy Building was a modernization job in Downtown LA run by a very colorful old timer we called "Huck." Huck had been around for years and years and was a great wrench. There was a big difference working construction with guys like Bud and John to working an inside job with Huck. We had long coffee and lunch breaks and the job just seemed to drag on. We just seemed to work around the edges of the work, rather than in the center. It was a little here, a little there. The jobs he ran always seemed like they would never end and they ran way over. When the job was finished, the Adjusters were in and out and the service guy got a job with few, if any, headaches.

Due to his age, the Company tried to give Huck inside jobs. There was a minor rub; he couldn't keep his mouth shut in front of the customer. More than a few times he was on the carpet in front of the Service Manager. A note here … in those days the service department ran the modernization jobs. Construction got them if the rails were replaced.

The Katy building had four gearless elevators installed by Llewellyn in the 20s. Otis later came along and modernized it again in the 50s. Our job was to install new controllers and replace the air doors with new door equipment. That meant the female elevator operators would soon be out of a job. It was touch and go for awhile but we all became friends. So friendly, in fact, when passenger traffic was slow, this good-looking operator with great legs would take her break and stand in the elevator opening while straddling the gap between the car and hall.

For some reason we could always find something to do directly beneath her in the walk-in pit.

I was there to help distribute the new door equipment and hoist the new controllers into the machine room. Huck and his Helper also needed a hand with some other work. We needed to replace the existing hitch plates on top of the cars with a Haughton hitch plate that contained load-weighing contacts. Before we started, the car top and hoist way had to be cleaned up.

The hoist way and car were covered with years and years of oily fuzz. Huck decided to use a Cadillac blower in lieu of a vacuum. These old Cadillac blowers put out such a blast of air, NASA could have used them to test the aerodynamics of the space shuttle. We started at the top of the hoist way working our way down, blowing off the fuzz and hoping we would sweep it up in the pit when finished.

This plan had one very serious flaw. The older cabs had very large exhaust fans mounted on top of the elevator. Boy, those things really put out a bunch of air or did they? Elevator fans are supposed to blow, but these guys sucked, and I mean really sucked.

It was just before lunch and a hot summer day. The elevators were packed with executives heading out for their two-martini lunch. We were unaware the car-top fans changed the scene in the lobby to that of a change of a shift at a West Virginia coal mine. Believe it or not, this day wasn't over yet. We just kept working as usual, after cleaning the hoist way, it was time to clean the pit but there wasn't the amount of fuzz we expected. Why...? The "fuzz" left the building with the white-shirted office workers right onto 5th street. That's right ... they were covered with soot. It would take awhile for the office to get wind of this fiasco.

We hung the car, secured the hoist ropes and started removing the old hitch plate. Problem was we couldn't break a bolt loose so a trip to the shack to retrieve the cutting torch was necessary. It was right after lunch and the part time coal miners were returning to work. The cars in the adjacent hoist ways were zipping by us nonstop. While cutting off the bolt a piece of red hot slag ignited the oily, fuzzy stuff on the side of a running car in the next hoist way. Damn, we had this blazing box of people rushing by us up and down at 500 feet per minute. Not a problem; Huck was always very safety conscious, so conscious he kept the fire extinguisher locked up in the shack so no one would steal it. I headed for the shack, Huck and his Helper swatted, blew, threw coffee, spit and would have probably pissed on the traveling fireball if they could. We got the fire out and later that day Huck assumed his usual position on the carpet in the Service Manager's office.

Huck's Helper on the Katy Building was a guy named Kelly. This Kelly was not "The Famous Kelly" mentioned later in this book, so we called him "Little Kelly." Kelly was kind of a flighty guy but a good Helper nonetheless. One day while working in the hoist way he inadvertently let his leg hang over into the adjacent hoist way. The car that lived in that hoist way whizzed by at 500 feet per minute and broke Kelly's leg into a zillion pieces. It must have hurt like hell, but he managed to crawl out onto the lobby. Writhing in pain with tears running down his face, he called for Huck, who finally sauntered up, called Kelly a "Pussy" and told him to get up and shake it off. Huck tried to get him to go for coffee in the shack, all the while telling Kelly he'll get over it in a few minutes. Eventually, after about 45 minutes Huck relented to calling an ambulance. Huck was right-on all right ... Kelly did shake it off ... after a week in the hospital and three months on crutches.

One day Kelly showed up in his wingtips for work. When we asked him why he was wearing his "Go to Meetin" shoes, he told us his work boots had been stolen. The deal was that his wife didn't allow him to wear his work boots in the house, so he used to park them on the front porch when he got home at night. The next morning when he went out to put his boots on, they were gone. Someone had stolen his old, smelly and, not to mention, oil-soaked boots right off his front porch. Just when I was really having fun, Bud wanted me back at FOB.

Back at FOB the Adjusters had the first bank of eight cars and they were finishing them up. On the other bank, we were completing the car top wiring, installing the comp ropes and painting. I had a little problem ... when I worked in the office I got to know the suits pretty well so when visiting our job site, they would walk right on by Bud to say hello to me and ask me, "How's the job going?" This created more than a little friction between Bud and me.

While at FOB, I worked alongside another card-carrying Helper, Mervin. Mervin was one of many Okies at Haughton who had fled the "Dust Bowl." These guys came off the farm where they learned how to fix stuff. They had to weld, fabricate and fix wiring on farm machinery and all kinds of mechanical stuff. Mervin was happy just being a Helper, and he was a damn good one at that. He was dependable, steady and a non-drinker. There was also Paul, a topnotch troubleshooter, his brother Keith, an ace Foreman and Adjuster who coined the term "Beginner and Advanced" for hacksaw blades. Beginner blades had lots of teeth which made it easier to start cut. Advanced blades had fewer teeth which made the cut more difficult. Iver was a right-on, hard-working Mechanic and then there was Sam, another quality Mechanic and finally "Okie John," our Construction Super.

There was a joke going around that you had to mow your boss's lawn in order to keep your job. This is no joke, but a true story. One Saturday, Okie John went over to Hugh's house. Hugh was the Regional Construction Manager. Okie John needed to discuss some business about the following workweek. When John showed up at Hugh's house, Hugh was out mowing his lawn. John and Hugh were talking when Hugh had a phone call and went back into the house. John was left standing by the lawn mower just when another Haughton elevator man drove by and saw him. Word spread faster than an Oklahoma prairie fire.

I was sent over to another Haughton job to load tools and excess material onto a truck to be returned to the shop. I had worked 108 West 6th Street a few months earlier. Bud had been the Foreman during the installation. West 6th was a ten-story building built in the 1900s. The four passenger cars were indirect roped water hydro's that traveled at around 500 feet per minute. Hard to believe a hydro could travel that fast. It was quite a site to watch those old jacks shoot up and down in a separate hoist way next to the elevator they served. This equipment was 70 years old, leaked like hell and squirted the water/oil mixture everywhere. Here's how it worked; the large water and soluble oil reservoirs were pressurized with air compressors which kept a constant pressure in the system. Los Angeles was full of these water hydros. We modernized some with the jack lying on its side some distance from the hoist way. There was also a ten-stop water hydro freight. Everything had to come out, right down to the guiderails. Four new gearless passenger elevators replaced the old passenger cars. A new geared freight replaced the old hydro freight. As usual, Bud and his crew did an excellent job.

Early in the installation we started by replacing the old water hydro freight with a new geared freight elevator. We loaded the new geared machine onto the old freight platform, ran the car up and everything was hunky-dory until we got to the top floor. While we were pushing the new machine off the old freight, it started drifting down. The machine was left teetering on the hoist way sill while the car was slowly disappearing down the hoist way. One problem was that there were large windows on the back of the hoist way. If the new machine teetered off the hoist way sill it would hit the sinking platform then tip through one of the windows and fall 10 floors down to the parking lot.

Our hero that day was Bob. While he was still on the car, he actually pushed the 4,000 pound machine back up onto the building landing. Just like "Big John," who, with a "Mighty Heave," held up the timbers to save other miners trapped in the mine ... "Big Bob, Big, Bad Bob." The new machine was sitting pretty on its pipe rollers out in the lobby, or was it? The building engineer came running down the hall like being chased by the Devil himself. "Hey you guys, that's only a hollow tile floor." Hollow tile floors will hold people, carts and just about anything except a 4,000 pound elevator machine sitting on two pipe rollers. Bob saved the day again by rounding up some planks so we could get the machine, along with its pipe rollers, on top of the plank. That way the weight was spread over a greater area. Later that day the machine was set.

There was a perk on this job that was a "Helpers Dream." A young lady working in the building really had a thing for elevator men. The locked walk-in barricades that were setup at each floor turned into a 4x4 motel room that charged by the hour. This particular young lady had no problem with servicing young Helpers behind the barricades. This went on for awhile until word leaked out. "If you guys get caught, you're down the Road." They got the picture and the at-work romances stopped. I think she then moved on to the Electricians.

I worked with Bob, the hero of 108 West 6th Street, on and off over the next several years. I found him to be, one of the greatest guys I've ever had the pleasure of knowing. Bob was quiet, strong as an ox with lots of hair; only problem … it was all in the wrong place. Matter of fact, the center of his head looked like a Q-ball. He was pretty self conscious about his baldness, so he combed the four-inch-long hair that grew on the side of his head to cover the shine. A Helper once told Bob, "If a fly tried to land on your head it would slip, fall on its ass and slide right off." One thing for sure, Bob had a very long fuse, but God help you if you got him pissed.

We used to have beers at a joint up on Sunset Boulevard which was a block away from the shop. You could bank on most of the Haughton crew being in there on payday. One payday it was business as usual. We were drinking beer, telling lies, pounding our chests and playing the bowling machine. Bob and another Mechanic were bowling on the machine when a Haughton truck driver picked up a ball, tossed it down the lane and spoiled the score for Bob and the other guy. The guy thought it was pretty funny. Bob politely asked him to knock it off. The driver didn't know who he was dealing with. Well, he did it again. "Bad Idea"… Bob just picked him up and tossed him down the alley with such force he wedged in the back of the machine. It took three of us to get him out of the inside of the machine. It was a strike!

It was hard to imagine during the Korean War at the Chosen Reservoir on a freezing December night in 1950 that this quiet man burned out the barrels of his Browning Automatic Rifle (BAR). This action along with other feats of valor won Bob a Silver Star, Bronze Star and a Purple Heart. Bob always said he would go out "With Fire Coming Out My Asshole."

He did just that, when later in his career his luck ran out. On a high rise job in Los Angeles Bob and his Helper were working on a newer skip that Haughton was using. These skips had no safeties and were powered by small winding drum machines mounted at the bottom landing. The skips used a three by eight-inch steel cable fed threw a block in the overhead and back down to the skip. The guys on the skip controlled it with a pendant station on a cable connected to the drum machine. No one was watching it while Bob and his Helper were working ten floors up the hoist way. The cable wound off the drum and broke. Bob and his Helper were in a ten floor free fall. While falling down the hoist way Bob made sure his Helper was laying flat on the skip to minimize his injuries. The skip hit the two-to-one sheave on the car frame sitting in the pit. Because the skip hit the sheave first, it broke in half and cushioned the fall. The Helper stayed on the skip and was not seriously hurt. Bob, on the other hand, didn't fare so well, he was still on his feet during the impact.

The impact threw him off the skip into the hoist way where he was wedged between the hoist way wall and the platform in the pit. Bob's recovery was a long ordeal. He couldn't walk for months. I and "Dirty John" paid him a visit and watched him get up unassisted and go to the bathroom for the first time since the accident. A year later Bob returned to work. Luck just wasn't on his side when a skill saw got away from him and ran across his arm. It took extensive surgery and rehabilitation before he could get back to work. Bob passed away a few years later. We lost a great comrade and hero. There are not enough and never will be enough men like Bob.

While returning to our cars after our weekly payday safety meeting at the beer joint on Sunset Boulevard, we encountered some fellow Haughton employees recreating in the parking lot. The parking lot was a shortcut which connected the shop and our favorite payday watering hole. We knew who they were because we recognized the Company car. The car with its windows all fogged up and bouncing around as if a champion bull riding contest was being held inside.

I recognized this car from my early days while working in the engineering department. The car had provided a shot in the arm for me and fellow draftsmen working in the engineering department. The driver had a parking spot next to our windows and gave us an excellent view almost every day.

The car and its occupants had different hours than the engineering department and as luck would have it, always arrived fifteen to twenty minutes after lunch when we were back at our parallel rulers. When the car entered the parking lot a sort of silent alarm went off in the department. You couldn't see or hear the alarm; it was more of just a feeling. The alarm was to alert the draftsmen of an upcoming leg shot. It was apparent the female occupant had never attended a finishing school of any kind. The passenger door would swing open; the knees swung around and exposed a space the size of a commuter lane on Interstate 5. This lady was definitely a subscriber to the new, but growing, underwear-optional movement. There was a collective groan emanating from the engineering department 15 to 20 minutes after lunch thanks to this car's arrival. We didn't groan too loud because alerting Fran to this after-lunch delight would spoil the whole spectacle.

On the larger Mod jobs we had a room that served as "The Shack." During the holidays, after-work parties were pretty common. Attendance wasn't mandatory so after round one, the group would usually dwindle down to the guys who were unmarried, unattached or had wives or girlfriends who didn't care whether they came home or not.

We were working a large modernization job at the County Hospital in Los Angeles during the holiday season. One member of our crew was Jake. He was a pretty nervous guy and for that reason, he picked up the handle "Jake the Snake." It was Christmas Eve and the remaining diehards were still hitting it hard and heavy in the shack. Jake had long since passed out and was scrunched up in a corner like a pretzel and looked like an unmade bed. The Foreman took pity on this crumpled mass of humanity and suggested we unfold him and find a more comfortable place for him to sleep it off.

Since the County Hospital had beds galore, I and another Helper were given the job of finding the perfect resting place for Jake. So that's exactly what we set out to do, piece of cake; all we had to do was find Jake an empty bed. My partner for this "Mission of Mercy" was a big, strong kid so with my help he was able to pick Jake up and sling him over his shoulder like a sack of potatoes. We left the shack, made a right turn down the hall to a semi-dark room and laid him out on a gurney.

For some reason, it was pretty cold in there so before leaving the room, we made sure Jake was completely covered up with a sheet. Upon returning to the party we were informed by the other guys who knew Jake well, that he would be out for some time. "Does he always pass out like this?" "Sometimes," was the answer. It just about always happens when he has a blow to the head.

"What blow to the head?" we asked. "The blow he took when his head hit the door jamb when you guys carried him out." The Foreman added, "Don't sweat it, I saw a guy hit him on the head with a pool cue hard enough to cold-cock Superman; he didn't even drop his beer. That blow wasn't even close and will only extend his nap by a few hours."

As the party progressed, everything was becoming one "Big Blur." The Foreman, while peering through his bloodshot eyes, asked, "What did you guys do with Jake?" "We put him on a gurney in the room down the hall and covered him up with a sheet because it's colder than hell in there," we said. He asked us to repeat that and, with an ear-to-ear grin he said, "If you guys stashed him where I THINK you did, we'd better get in there and check on him before something really bad happens." "What can happen?" we asked. "Ever hear of an autopsy?" "Don't get it," we replied. "You'll damn well get it when we get there," answering with a smirk. So what was left of the crew staggered down the hall to check on "Good ole Jake." With the state we were in we were lucky to find Jake at all. County General was built in the late 20s and word has it, it was built in such a way so disease couldn't spread within its walls and believe me, it couldn't. A germ couldn't directly travel from one place to another without taking stairs, elevators or exiting the building and using a different entrance. With all the mysterious doors and rooms, it was best to never enter without knocking or while alone, fearing we might interrupt some medical professionals such as Dr. Frankenstein, Dr. Jekyll or maybe even a Mr. Hyde.

When we entered the darkened room, "Which one?" the Foreman asked. "Don't remember," we said. One of the brighter guys in our group turned up the lights and it became crystal clear where we were . . ."The Morgue." We soon found out that Jake's resting place was way more than he or we bargained for. The first thing we noticed was that Jake had company . . . It was the holidays and actually he had quite a bit of company. There were five or six other guys in there, but instead of the work boots like Jake's poking out from under the sheet, they had bare feet sticking out with a white tag attached to their big toe . . . It wasn't all that difficult to spot Jake as there was only one sheeted, snoring, shaking, non-toe-tagged, boot-wearing guy in the room. After a positive ID, we added another sheet, tucked him in and bid a drunken good night to his still-shaking body.

Just before heading back to the party some wise guy found a toe tag and attached it to Jake's boot lace. On one side of the toe tag we inscribed "Here lies Jake The Snake, One Hell Of An Elevator Man." On the other side, we wrote "Live Body, please do not autopsy."

We never did find out what Jake thought upon awakening. Nor did we bother to inquire.

After the holidays, the crew split up and went to other jobs so I didn't see Jake for another year or so. I asked him about that memorable Christmas Eve and it seems I'm the only guy who remembered it. Good thing, maybe yes, maybe no . . . !

One thing for sure ... "Jake the Snake" became famous that Christmas Eve.

John was a man of many names. To name a few; Dangerous John, The German, Uncle John and Dirty John (DJ).

DJ was born and raised in Northern Indiana. During WWII he served his country as a crew chief in the Army Air Corps in England. DJ had been in the business for a long time and had worked with a lot of the old-timers. He told us about these old guys during breaks and lunchtime. He worked his way up from Helper to Foreman. He pushed some of the largest jobs Haughton had done in LA and Las Vegas. Las Vegas was his favorite place to work.

He had been Frank's (our Superintendent) Helper some years back and told us about when they were working on an old elevator at the YWCA in Downtown LA. The elevator had one of its openings disabled with clothing lockers stacked in front of the entrance. That particular floor just happened to be the women's shower and dressing room. DJ and the other Helper found an unexpected form of entertainment. If they spread the hoist way doors at the bottom then a whole world of older, naked alabaster-skinned women in various poses were in plain view. As the views prevailed themselves the sweat beads formed on the young Helpers' foreheads. Laughing had to be contained so the boys would retreat to the back of the platform to avoid detection. The Mechanics finally figured out something was going on and recalled the Helpers and elevator to the basement and demanded an explanation for the loss of productivity. Shortly there were two more sweating, giggling men in the dark watching naked women showering and undressing.

One day during our bull sessions in the shack during lunch, DJ was revisiting his teenage years when the story he was entertaining us with caught the attention of an older Helper, Dale.

Dale and DJ came from the same town in Northern Indiana and even knew the same woman. As DJ's story unfolded, he told of visiting an older woman and having intimate relations with her while her husband was at work. As Dale listened intently his color, not to mention his mood, began to change and not for the better, I might add. "You Son-of-a Bitch, that was my first wife." Silence filled the shack as Dale stood up and approached DJ. A smile broke out on his face as he muttered, "Thanks buddy, I hated that woman and was trying to get rid of her; because of you I finally made it."

Dale had another reason to have hard feelings toward DJ because his brother was seriously injured on one of his jobs. They were hoisting a machine up the hoist way with a chain fall powered by one of Haughton's large catheads. The free side of the pull chain was forming a loop and his brother reached into the hoist way to center the load. The moving loop of chain took a wrap on his upper arm just below the shoulder and pulled him into the hatch with such force it pulled his skin and flesh down to the elbow. The crew stopped the cathead, untangled the chain and pulled him out of the hoist way and called for help. His injuries had been so debilitating that he was never able to return to work.

Working for DJ as a grunt was like working for a favorite uncle. You were pretty much on your own; if you saw it needed to be done and did it, everything was cool. There was an upside and a downside to this work ethic. A few mistakes were made; on one job we painted all the governors. Why? They didn't match the rest of the machine equipment that had already been painted. Hey! They really looked great, but there was one major rub. The Adjusters had already calibrated them in preparation for the safety tests which were to be held the next day. Our paint job was very thorough and pretty but unfortunately the safety tests had to be canceled. A note here, elevator guys don't really use strokes to apply the paint, it's more like a dip and stab action. I really believe there is equipment I painted in the 60s that probably hasn't dried yet.

DJ was not only a great guy to work for, but also a lot of fun. He watched out for his people. One of the best examples I can remember was when a Helper charged into the shack with tears in his eyes. This Helper had been around for some time. He was a big tough guy and definitely not subject to turning on the waterworks. As the story goes, the Helper was installing a gutter cover in one of the machine rooms when he dropped a screw into a running gearless machine. This machine belonged to an elevator that had just been turned over and was in service. The screw hit the machine, bounced into the space between the field pieces and the armature, sparks flew, the DC overload tripped and the elevator ground to a halt. Fortunately, the elevator was unoccupied. DJ handed him a rag from the rag box so he could wipe his eyes, and proceeded to settle him down. "Don't sweat it, we'll figure something out." Together they headed for the machine room to assess the damage. The Helper had a reason to be crying. The machine was trashed and would have to be disassembled; the damaged field pieces and armature would have to be replaced. No easy task, for this was a Big Ass Haughton #40 Machine that weighed in at around 12,000 pounds. Being the clever guy DJ was, he looked at the damage and within seconds came up with a solution to this dilemma. There was an air conditioning duct that ran right over the top of the machine. He removed one of the screws from the duct, looked at it and said. "That's the son-of-bitch right here that screwed up our machine." The screw was a pretty good match and became a perfect match after a couple of blows with a single jack. Right or wrong the sheet metal contractor's insurance company footed the bill for the repair job.

Back then we were doing tons of modernizations and John always kept his eyes open for hidden treasures. We tore out solid bronze doors that weighed up to two hundred pounds. Some had ten coats of old paint that covered the bronze. Another example of hidden treasures was the beautiful marble John found in the trash pile. He had us scoop it up and load it in his truck. Happy as a clam, he cut it up and put it all over his house. Seeing his work reminded us of the "Taj Mahal." All was great until he found out why it had been tossed. It became very clear where it came from on the first cold night of the year. After closing up his house and turning on the heater, a distinct odor began to permeate his happy home. His treasure turned out to be the pieces of marble that separated the urinals in the men's bathroom. Seventy-five years of misguided pee was seeping out of John's prize.

Haughton, like all companies, ran out of work from time to time and would have to find work for their best people. I was lucky enough to be working with "Uncle John" when the last big job finished up. They usually had a hydro or two where they could stash a crew.

After finishing a large job John became pretty laid back, so laid back in fact I thought he'd dissolve.

I met John at a coffee shop out in Redlands. After mass quantities of coffee, I rode with him over to the job. As we drove on by the job John said, "Looks like a nice little job," and we headed for the nearest beer joint and spent the rest of the day drinking beer, shooting pool and eating Polish Sausage sandwiches before heading for the motel.

Day two started the same as day one, only this time we actually stopped at the job, looked in the pit and up the hoist way. John told the General Contractor (GC) he would have to get the pit cleaned out so we could get started. Then it was off to beer, pool, darts and Polish Sausage sandwiches.

On day three we opened the gang box and got out the prints. John looked them over and it was off to beer, pool and Polish Sausage sandwiches.

On day four we unloaded John's tools and started laying out the installation. Day four just happened to be the Thursday prior to a three-day weekend. Around noon we headed for home.

Out of town Mondays are always tough after a three-day weekend. This Monday we found all of our equipment covered with brown coat. Brown coat is a base troweled onto the metal lath prior to the white coat (finish). We looked up the plaster Foreman to piss a bitch about the state of our stuff. This guy was less than sympathetic. Fact is, he couldn't have cared less. He gave us a line like, "A different crew needed the money and worked over the weekend." John wouldn't let up and followed him out to his truck just to watch him leave. "Forget it, don't worry, we'll get these guys."

The rest of the day was spent cleaning up the plasterers mess. John called the office and was told they would try to back-charge the GC. The problem with the GC was that he was just a former "ding batter" (house builder) and had never done a job of any size, especially one with an elevator!

A couple of days later the plasterers returned to the job and went about their work as if nothing ever happened. John's mood changed to one of gleeful apprehension. The next day he showed up with a small paper sack. He never brought his lunch, so I asked him what was in the sack. "Just wait, Jim, you're going to love this one; just hang on and I'll show you the way elevator men get even."

While working in the hoist way John kept his secret bag close at hand, waiting for the all-clear. The time came early in the day when I found out what he had up his sleeve. He had instructed me to keep an eye on the plasterers and to tell him when they were applying the brown coat on the metal lath. Also, to inform him when they had a fresh wheelbarrow of brown coat and were not around. At 10 a.m., while they were down at the gut wagon, we carried out our mission. Darting in and out of doorways, like on a commando mission, we found our prize, a wheelbarrow full of brown coat that even had a mixing hoe inserted in the mix. While John was emptying the contents of the bag, he instructed me to quickly mix it all up. Done with our clandestine act, we went to coffee.

"What was that?" I asked John, "rye grass seed," was his reply. He looked at my normally-confused face and noticed it was really confused. He explained we would probably be long gone before the fruit of our labor surfaced. And, I do mean surface … rye grass seed loves the moist brown coat and will grow like hell. The plasterers would have already applied the white or finish coat over the brown coat hopefully before the painters accepted the wall. I say "hopefully" because our beef was with the plasterers, not the painters. The rye grass would grow through the white coat and turn into the most beautiful horizontal lawn that would make any proud homeowner "green" with envy.

I had a chance to work with Larry, one of the Adjusters. Larry adjusted the West Coast Hydro's we manufactured in Glendale. The Company had set him up with a utility truck and a trailer that hauled the test weights. This setup was a very self-contained operation.

The Haughton construction department was setup with a couple of Superintendents managing the traction jobs and one Superintendent, Mel, who managed the hydro jobs. He usually had five crews just installing the "West Coast Hydro's."

This separation of installations extended to the field. The hydro guys usually worked out in the zones which meant a fatter paycheck. The traction guys normally worked downtown in zone one and had to pay for parking which was not covered by the "Standard Agreement."

When the hydro work slowed down, the hydro crews worked the traction jobs, all the while taking lots of guff from the traction guys. The traction guys looked down on the hydro guys and the hydro guys regarded the traction guys as bull workers. The Hydro guys were easy to spot due to the color of their boots, in fact, if you could wring them out, the result would provide enough oil to fill a two-stop hydro tank. The traction guys had their own trade mark, the rope-shaped groove in the insole of their boots. This groove was caused by the lowering of skips by hand for short distances. Rather than wrap the short length around the falls, it was easier to step on the free line and control the speed of the descent. During the longer, faster descents the rope could get the boot pretty damn hot.

Back to Larry, he was a Canuck who grew up in Winnipeg and had great stories about "The Great White North" and how he worked on the caravans that crossed the frozen tundra, hauling supplies for the mines and the isolated settlements. He also served with the RAF during WWII. He never talked about his war experiences until one night.

I was his Helper when we adjusted several jobs in Santa Barbara. He had the hydro adjustment wired. We would setup the door locks, limit switches and the operator. These elevators were always wired for sound-powered phones which we used for the adjusting procedure. Larry would ride the car and give me instructions on tweaking the valves. He knew these valves so well, there were times when he'd come back and say, "You didn't turn the adjustment like I told you." He was always right.

The local gin mill where the elevator guys hung out was a place called "Le Johns." This place suited Larry just fine because he loved his scotch. One night, after bending our elbows and getting thoroughly hammered, we returned to our motel room to crash and burn.

While laying in our beds in the dark he started talking about the RAF. He told of leaving Canada for Britain in the early 40s to enlist. He became a crew member on a bomber that flew night bombing raids over Europe. During these raids his crew had to fly through incredible anti-aircraft fire, fight off German night fighters and tend to fellow wounded crewmen. I couldn't see his face but could tell by the tone of his voice how emotional he became. He told two stories so well I could visualize every frightening moment. The bomber he flew in is now on display in a Museum in London because it survived more combat missions than any other bomber of its type. Larry and others like him saved the world during those dark nights over "Fortress Europe."

Toward the end of Larry's career, he had a serious accident that came close to costing him his life. He was answering a call on a hydro freight in a manufacturing plant. It was raining like hell when he entered the building from the parking lot. The machine was in a fenced off section of the plant. He was already wet when he leaned inside the machine and spotted a broken wire. For some reason, he grabbed it. That wire was 220 Volts AC hot. He became paralyzed in place. He was unable to move and all that worked were his eyes. He later told us he watched the plant workers walking by just a few yards away. "I thought, please look at me." Fortunately after an undetermined amount of time one of the workers spotted him and rushed into the fenced enclosure and pulled the disconnect. The doctors at the emergency room said he couldn't have lasted much longer. Larry spent some time in the hospital recuperating and after some time at home he was able to return to work.

Larry worked several years before retiring and passed away a few years later. His funeral looked like an Elevator Man's Convention.

CHAPTER SIX
Kelly

It was a cold morning at the north end of the San Fernando Valley as I stood waiting for "Legendary Mechanic, Thomas John Kelly," affectionately known as TJ, Kelly or just plain Tom. Kelly pulled up in his '63 Chevy wagon and invited me in out of the cold. By the time I slid my tail into the passenger seat I remembered where my channel locks and screwdriver were. The latter had ripped a long gash in the seat when I slid into the car. Was this a great way to start the first day with the famous Kelly?

Kelly was unperturbed and went on to tell a story about when he started a new job. He jumped into his new boss's Cadillac, which had leather seats, with a linoleum knife in his back pocket. And then he offered me a cup of coffee from his ten-gallon thermos.

Prior to that moment, you couldn't have driven a needle up my ass with a jack hammer.

While Kelly unloaded his tools, I had a chance to eyeball him. After hearing all the stories, I expected a giant of a man. Instead, here was this little guy about 5'4" wearing tan Levies, a sport shirt, Wellington boots and sporting a well-groomed goatee.

We entered the building, looked in the hoist way and then opened the standard Haughton grey and yellow gang box. The job at hand was a six-stop geared elevator in a science building at San Fernando Valley State College. Most of the heavy work was done. Rails, machine, pit structures and machine room equipment had been set.

Over the next couple of weeks, we installed the cwt frame, the car frame and deflector sheave and then roped it all together. While building the car frame, Kelly opened up the hardware bag to find all the bolts were bent, so he tossed them. We needed hardware right now, so Kelly called the shop and ordered new hardware. What we didn't know was that Haughton started using offset bolts in lieu of hillside washers. We sure heard about this repeatedly from the other crews for months to come.

I started unpacking some boxes when this guy armed with a clip board and camera approached me and started asking questions about the elevator. He informed me that he was a reporter for the school paper and was writing an article about the new building. I informed him that I was not allowed to answer any questions due to my grunt status, and he would have to talk to Kelly. Kelly was standing over by the open hoist way. As this guy approached him, he turned and jumped into the hoist way while emitting a bloodcurdling scream. The poor reporter dropped his camera, clipboard and pencil. After gathering up his stuff he headed for the stairwell never knowing Kelly's fate. Kelly, in his death plunge, had simply slid down the three-to-three rope falls and landed on the waiting skip below. We never saw that reporter again.

The end of the workday was as predictable as the tightening of a nun's bun on Good Friday. We would find shelter in a local beer joint while waiting for the LA traffic to subside. The intersection at Tampa and Ventura had three such places. One place was pretty large with a long bar, tables, pool tables and bathrooms in the back. Back in those days the barmaids revealed as much skin as the law allowed. The afternoon barmaid wore a very small bikini. She had a great body but the face would make a freight train take a dirt road. After thoroughly checking her out Kelly remarked, "All That Tree to Raise That Prune."

Pool and cold beer occupied our afternoons. It was pretty damn hot out in the valley, as a matter of fact, we wouldn't even open the first beer bottle; we just dropped it in like a capsule. Kelly was an excellent pool shooter and a good sport as well. One afternoon I found out just how tough this little guy was. We were playing pool and this big guy challenged the table. I lost the game, so Kelly and the new guy started playing. Kelly never played for money, just for fun or showing off for a crowd. For some reason, this new guy thought he was "Minnesota Fats" and took his game very seriously. Kelly embarrassed him game after game which pissed this guy off. He was so pissed off he made mistake #1 and walked around the table and punched Kelly right in the mouth. Kelly stepped back, looked at the guy and said, "Hey man, this is just a friendly game so why in the hell did you hit me in the mouth?"... Mistake #2 ... the guy hit Kelly again. Kelly was on him like a cat. Seconds later "Minnesota Fats" was slumped over a chair whimpering like a little kid. "Enough," we told Kelly and coaxed him back to the bar with a promise of beer and praise. All was quiet until someone noticed Kelly was missing from the bar. Looking back at the pool tables, we saw Kelly finishing the guy off. It finally ended when we pulled Kelly off and carried the bloody, defeated and embarrassed combatant out to the parking lot.

We became good friends with the owner of this particular joint. One afternoon, much to the owner's surprise, we celebrated my 21st birthday there. Kelly and I had been drinking at his place for the last three months.

Across Ventura Boulevard was a joint with the raunchiest barmaid in the Valley. And that's saying a lot. While we were entering this establishment on a hot Valley afternoon and packing a genuine "Death Valley" thirst, a hardhat came bouncing out the front door spilling yellow liquid all over the parking lot. Once inside, we found out the barmaid had grabbed this guy's hardhat, knelt down behind the bar and pissed in it. Kelly, not to be outdone started with raw eggs in his beer and then graduated to one of his most famous acts. He would take a bite of a beer glass and slowly chew it into tiny little pieces. This continued until just the thick bottom of the glass was left. No, he didn't swallow.

Across Tampa from this joint was another place where the main attraction was bottomless barmaids. We went in there a couple of times and it was no big deal. They wore lingerie with no panties. It was kind of like watching a woman through a shower curtain. Besides all the patrons were checking bush so Kelly had a tough time entertaining everybody. Needless to say, we didn't spend much time there.

We turned the science building over to the Adjuster and moved on to the next one at The Bush Brewery in the San Fernando Valley.

The Bush Brewery job was pretty well along when we unloaded Kelly's tools. It was summer and the Valley was as hot as it gets. Inside the building was a constant 40 degrees. There was no room in the building for our material so we brought it in from 105 degrees to 40 degrees as we needed it.

We hung doors, installed the door operator, set the geared machine, set the machine room equipment and completed all the waterproof wiring. Overall, there was about a month's work.

Talk about conditions. This job had the best because we were working in the same building with "The Brewery Workers Union." These guys had written into their contract a seven-minute beer break on the hour. It didn't take Kelly long to win friends and influence people enough to get an unlimited invitation to their break room. The room looked like most break rooms with one very significant exception ... "Tapped Beer." So each day after the coffee break at 10 a.m. we would rinse out our thermos cups so not to pollute the beer with a coffee taste. Three times a day we would visit the tap room with our sanitized coffee cups ... this job definitely ran over!

As per usual, the time we had after work was spent at the local bar, rehydrating. The closest bar to the job was a gin mill. We normally avoided hard-liquor establishments because the clientele was older and more difficult for Kelly to entertain. Hard-liquor bars pretty much have the same patrons. Examples are: The poor guy in the corner dying of some unknown incurable disease. You always have to buy this guy a drink. When you do, he looks up and gives you a slight nod as if that drink is the last one he will ever see. Then there is the resident bad guy who gets his rocks off by beating up old drunks (he always steered clear of us). Then there's the resident barfly, age unknown but definitely her speedometer is rolled way back. The rest of the patrons had been occupying their barstools since the place was built. In this particular place, there were pictures on the wall of when the place opened in the 50s. The people in the pictures are the same people sitting on the same stools with us today.

On the bar were the hottest red peppers known to man. Kelly could drop those things down like gumdrops and wouldn't even make a face. One afternoon our Construction Manager, Hugh, stopped with us and thought he could go head-to-head with Kelly in a pepper-eating contest. Kelly 10, Hugh 1. Hugh didn't say a word for 10 minutes.

Kelly and I parted company. Kelly went on to another job in LA. I headed to Las Vegas.

CHAPTER SEVEN
Viva Las Vegas

We all shared an apartment off the strip in Las Vegas, which saved us money and made it easier for the guys who were coming and going. I arrived one afternoon to find DJ braced up behind a big ass one-half inch drill motor drilling a two inch hole in the side of the apartment's refrigerator. The food was in the trash can. As DJ drilled away I asked, "What's up John?"... He replied, with a grin, "Well, I just put a tapper in here; all those trips to the store for more beer really cuts into our drinking time." From that day forward we always had plenty of cold beer on tap, no food of course; the rest of the space was reserved for spare cold kegs. Who needs food anyway?

While working in Las Vegas, our weekends were spent shooting pool and drinking beer. We went over to pick up another Mechanic, Rex. Unlike the other Mechanics, whose wives and girlfriends were back home, Rex had his wife with him. At his place we found him working on his motorcycle in the front yard. His son was helping out, by taking the bolts Rex had removed and driving them into the ground with a hammer. One of the guys said,

"Hey man, you gonna let him do that?" Like the great father he was, Rex immediately disciplined the boy by saying, "Don't do that," and that was all. I mean that was it! To this day, we wonder where that kid, now grown up, is serving his time. The little bugger did come in handy; Rex brought him in more than once to install handrail nuts.

Rex may not have had the perfect kid but he sure had the perfect wife. He cleaned up and while leaving with us, he said to his wife, "I'm going out with these guys to drink beer and shoot pool, I don't know when I'm coming home and by the way, while I'm out, wash my truck and don't leave any streaks on it like you did the last time."

There was an eerie silence as we looked at each other in disbelief, if only our girlfriends and wives could take lessons from this amazing woman. Rex, just like the song, was a very "Macho, Macho Man." Some years later, while hoisting a rail, it came back at him, hitting him in the chest. The machined end of guiderails is sharper than hell and can cause a lot of damage. The impact did just that. He went to the ER with a very large jagged gash. The doctor told him it would take a whole lot of stitches to close the wound to prevent a serious scar. He quizzed the MD and asked, "What if I don't get it sewed up?" The MD replied, "You will have a very noticeable scar on your chest." "That's great," Rex quipped, and left.

Las Vegas was a fun place to work. We would start early to avoid the heat and end up at the lake in the afternoon. Dirty John had a boat on the lake and we spent our after-work hours drinking beer, telling lies and it was business as usual. Kelly had arrived in town and started joining us in the afternoon. He was his old self, would do anything for a laugh. This one went down in Elevator Man's History.

It was a typical hot, sunny afternoon at the marina where Dirty John kept his boat. The marina had two live-bait tanks, one contained minnows, the other waterdogs. Waterdogs are one of the ugliest critters God put on this earth. They were salamanders about three inches long, with horns all over their body. As ugly as they were, bass loved them. The minnows were the first victims. Dirty John would swoosh his hand around the tank, grab one, throw it into his mouth and wash it down with beer. Kelly, not to be outdone, would grab two or three and do the same. Pretty soon these guys were grabbing handfuls of the little fish and swilling them down with beer. If they had their stomachs x-rayed, they would probably look like an aquarium or one of those screen savers you get for your computer. The contest seemed to be dead until Kelly decided to break the impasse. He reached into the waterdog tank, grabbed a poor unfortunate creature by the tail and dropped it down his throat, head first. Okay, Kelly you win, let's go back to telling lies. The waterdog had its own idea. Kelly was doing fine, laughing and joking just like the typical Kelly.

We were all still eyeing him to see what would be the final outcome of his last "Go Ya One Better." He started to do this convulsive retching and turned kind of green. He got up, ran down the dock, dove in headfirst, landed on his belly and regurgitated the, "You're not gonna get me," waterdog. This brave little amphibian spewed from Kelly's mouth, hit the deck running, and jumped into the water. You bet no "Big Mouth Bass" will ever screw with this little escapee. To this day there are reports of large pets, water skiers, swimmers and even small boats mysteriously disappearing on Lake Mead. I'll bet you "Dimes to Donuts" Kelly's waterdog is the culprit.

We were working in Las Vegas with a familiar crew setup. "Big Bill" was the Foreman and we were the grunts ... Mike, Ernie and me. Night life in Las Vegas was great. We were out every night. One night the boys ran into Bill's wife at Honest John's (the preferred watering hole). Bill's wife was waiting for Bill, but he was very late. The boys sat down with his wife and proceeded to have a few drinks with her. These guys were funny and very entertaining. By the time Bill arrived the threesome was well on its way to getting smashed. This scenario would have been okay with anyone except Bill. He was a very jealous man, I mean a very, very jealous man. He was extremely pissed and the boys beat feet in a hurry.

It was difficult for the boys to avoid Bill on the jobsite but, using more stealth than an F18, they somehow managed. Being the jokesters they were, they just couldn't leave it alone. They were working in the hoist way and saw Bill's shadow on the wall. Bill had opened the hoist way doors two floors above them. He was checking on them but did not know they knew he was watching their every move. It was time to get him again. "Hey Ernie, what are we doing tonight?" Mike answered, "Well, I don't know, maybe we should take out Bill's old lady, she was the greatest." That was it; they could hear the doors slam and knew, sure as hell, Bill was on his way down the stairs to deal out some Big Bill retribution. Mike and Ernie left early that Friday. Good thing it was a weekend and Bill had a chance to cool off. On Monday, everything was back to normal.

In the 60s, the uniform of the day was a pair of 501s, medium top work boots, a Penncraft colored tee shirt and a Company shirt furnished by the Company. Haughton's shirt was green and had our name and Company logo attached. The Haughton logo was a round black and orange patch with a large "H" in the center. From a distance it looked like a small pumpkin.

Bobby was younger, single, very handsome and an all-around nice guy. Working in Las Vegas for him was like being a "kid in a candy store." That town was full of unbelievably good-looking women. Bobby had been working in town for about a month when he hooked up with this beautiful showgirl. She was crazy about Bobby and he likewise. We were all friends with Bobby and his girl. We spent a lot of time in the clubs, bars and restaurants.

The Company sent Bobby back to LA for a few months to work on a large job. He flew back to Las Vegas every weekend to spend time with his girlfriend.

I forgot to mention, Bobby was a very jealous guy and this is where the real story begins.

On occasion we would have a drink with Bobby's girlfriend during the week while he was working in LA. The longer he worked out of town the more pissed off he became about our socializing with the love of his life and always warned us not to go too far. There was absolutely no hanky-panky at all, but we managed to get to him when we gave his girl friend a "Pumpkin Patch." She agreed with our plan and sewed the patch on a very intimate piece of underwear in a very intimate place.

The girlfriend picked Bobby up at the Airport and naturally, after being apart for all of five days, the two rushed home to spend some personal time together.

Bobby didn't speak to us for a couple of weeks.

CHAPTER EIGHT
San Diego

The First National Bank would soon be the tallest building in San Diego. First National had 30 landings, six 700 FPM gearless passenger cars, one 500 FPM gearless service car and one three-stop vault elevator.

Material had to be off-loaded and stored quickly. First came a semi loaded with rail brackets in 55 gallon drums, and then came the first of several flatbed trailers with the rails. All of this material had to be unloaded and stored undercover on the same day it arrived. The barrels of rail brackets were unloaded and stored. We used hand trucks to roll the barrels onto the outside material hoist to be distributed on the upper landings. The first shipment of rails was unloaded off the flatbed using the building derrick, then placed on dollies and snaked into the building. We had to maneuver around many obstacles to get as close to the hoist ways as possible. During all the unloading, storing and distribution of material, the class structure among Helpers was nonexistent. We all had to bust our asses to get the job done.

To start with, our crew consisted of two crews of local San Diego guys and then Bud, along with two crews from LA. Bud coined the term "San Diego Pussies;" that sure as hell didn't win him any popularity contests. I don't think Bud really gave a damn. San Diego was a great city and still had a small town atmosphere. The LA guys were used to working big jobs like First National and we prided ourselves on how hard we worked and played. The locals, on the other hand, came off the out-of-work list for the San Diego Chapter of Local 18. Work came for them when a major company came to town for large elevator installations or when the smaller independent companies got busy and needed extra help. The local companies tended to be very tight knit and kept family members and friends employed first. The local guys were good Mechanics, a little older and definitely not used to working for a Foreman like Bud on a large fast-paced job like First National.

The local guys had "Home Field" advantage and could go home at night for dinner, sleep in their own bed and had a wife to pack their lunch. We, on the other hand, ate lunch off the gut wagon, drank together, ate dinner in greasy spoons and all lived in the same place.

We found lodging up the street from First National in a one-half star establishment called the "New Pantlin Hotel." You can imagine what the "Old Pantlin" was like. Checking in and riding up to our room with the rest of our crew was like my first skip ride at FOB. Why in the hell did all of those big elevator men want to get on this little "Early American" phone-booth-sized elevator at the same time? I waited for it to come back and get me.

First off, and of the utmost urgency, we had to locate a watering hole with pool tables that catered to hardhats like us. In the interim we hung out at a gin mill across the street from the hotel. It was frequented by nice, quiet and very well-behaved locals. In just a few weeks our crew would change all that. We were finally 86'd. Just four blocks down "B" Street, our scouts found a beer joint to our liking. After the crew was kicked out, a few of us were still able to drop in for an occasional late night pool game and nightcap.

The green Helpers were delegated to the "Rail Pile." We had to carry the main guiderails to the elevator lobby to clean off the Cosmoline with solvent and then file the joints so they would fit together when stacked. These main guiderails weighed in at 16 pounds per foot and weighed 256 pounds each. There is no way to carry a rail easily. To begin with, if you are the guy in front you have to carry the rail alongside your body and you can't carry it by the end because of the sharp machined edges. Along with the rails there were 150 lb bundles of fish plates that had to be unbolted, cleaned, filed and then bolted to one end of the rails. We made good money in those days but later the orthopedic surgeons made a lot more attempting to repair the damage.

While we were preparing the rails for installation, the building was going up around us. Bud ordered lumber for the targets and skips. He always used select grade. The work was starting to get scary. We traveled up to the 10th floor on the Alimak then two more floors on eight-foot wide ladders built by the carpenters. Then we pulled the lumber up to the 12th landing using ropes. The ironworkers would plank over the open steel as it went up. They were usually a couple of floors behind the steel erection and connecting with the planking. Our job was to build targets over the open hoist ways. Believe me, when you're up there for the first time, you never get off your butt. Matter of fact, some of the patrons at the bar that afternoon jokingly asked, "You elevator guys have digestive problems?" This stemmed from the red-brown stain up the back of our pants. The targets were built and piano wire was dropped down 12 floors to the pits where the rest of the crew had built corresponding targets. We dropped the piano wire down to the pits where they were connected to 50 lb weights. Now the whole deal was ready to layout. Everything had to be aligned to the "Nuts." Using the layout provided by the factory, we first aligned three cars on one bank then cars across the nonexistent lobby to the other three cars. Using 100 ft tapes, we setup bank-to-bank dimensions and then triangulated the six cars from the extreme corners to square all six cars up. All this setting up was a chore due to the fact that there was nothing but open steel up there. The first Mechanic and Bud would then check dimensions at each floor to verify we had proper clearance to install the elevators. While up on top, we also installed the rigging so we could hang our skips and start stacking the main rails. I was tightening up the Crosby clips on a piece of cable while straddling a four inch beam and using all the vacuum my rectum could provide. I heard, "Excuse me buddy," when this ironworker, with his spud wrenches and tool bag, leapfrogged right over me, landed on his feet and kept going. The Iron heads didn't like any other trade in their territory. As the job started they always looked at us as outsiders. Over time friends were made and we got along just fine … until it came time to set machine beams. They got a little antsy about work they considered to be their own. It is our work but the Ironworkers were facing layoffs because their work was winding down.

We set the pit channels and first main rails so we could start building our skips. During this type of work, there was all matter of stuff coming down our hoist ways. The guy who dropped the stuff was usually so far above you that by the time you heard "Headache," it was too late. Our skips were still the same as the ones elevator men had been using for 50 years. They were constructed of plywood, 2 x 4s, no safeties and no guardrails. They had to be safe because we built, rigged and had to work off them.

Bud setup one crew exclusively to install the service car. That car would be the first inspected and turned over for the contractors use.

The skips were built, hung and the crews started running rails in all seven hoist ways. The rail pile got a lot busier; Bud put on two more crews, and we starting stacking rails. The experienced Helpers ran the catheads in the basement. There was one crew per hoist way on adjacent skips. The grunts dragged the rails over to the hoist way and attached them to the free line to be hoisted up to the crews on the skips waiting above. The crews on the skips stacked one rail per side. Then they drilled holes in the building steel and bolted on the next bracket. Then they dropped in ¼" of shims, tightened the bolts, moved up and stacked two more rails. The grunts down in the lobby damn well better have the rails ready to go or Bud would tear you a new one. This all went on for a couple of days then the crews on the skips moved across the lobby and started the process all over again.

We had clear hoist ways up to the 10th floor and would have six more floors soon. As the upper hoist ways opened up Bud put on two more crews. One crew came from LA and the other from San Diego. The job became a whole lot more interesting. The Mechanic from LA was Kelly!

Kelly took over the topside work as "First Mechanic." As usual, his talent as a great Mechanic, and not to mention his pranks and humor, would keep all of us very entertained while we worked.

Kelly became buds with this gung-ho ironworker who was quite a guy. To begin with he and Kelly would run the stairs to the top of the building every morning. Kelly raced no matter how hung over he was. Thinking back over all those years, I never knew Kelly to suffer from the effects of "Them Bad Ole Demon Spirits."

Kelly and this Iron head would also test each other's nerves by walking out on the open steel on their heels, 12 and then later 30 floors over "B" Street. I saw them with two-inches left off their heels still remaining on the steel beam. You have to understand here, this is the very top of the building on open steel and nothing on any side except air.

We ran rails, built car frames and installed comp sheaves. All along Kelly continued to entertain, not just for us but for the San Diego public as well. One of his most cherished possessions was his rubber barf. I'll bet he kept it in a safety deposit box when not in use. He would buy a sandwich and soda off the gut wagon then sit outside the barricades at the corner of 5th and B to eat his lunch. He'd lay his rubber barf on the sidewalk, pour a little soda on it to give it a fresh look, and while he had all the pedestrians' attention, he'd dip his sandwich in and take a big bite.

The only time I ever saw Kelly rattled was when he was showing off and doing a high-wire act, walking up a cable that supported the derrick 20 floors in the air. The Iron heads were using the derrick to place a very large beam. The beam didn't fit the first time, so they raised it about 10 feet and let it go. The beam came down with a resounding crash. The cable with Kelly aboard started whipping around and throwing him off. Kelly grabbed the cable and slid down to a beam below.

Kelly showed up late one morning with a large bruise on his forehead. We found out he parked his '63 Chevy wagon on the street near the job and slept in its zippered car top carrier. This was a very handy crash pad after our evenings of after-work beers. He usually unzipped the carrier, stuck his head out, did a back flip and landed on his feet. One morning he slept in and didn't climb out before the pedestrian traffic got busy. There was a problem with his exit. During the bailout, his belt hung up on the carrier's zipper which left him hanging upside down with his forehead kissing the sidewalk. Fortunately, some good samaritan passerby unhooked him and saved the day.

We had another lunch spot that served a quick, hot and good lunch. The Chicken Pie Shop was right across the street from the job, so with only a half hour for lunch, it was perfect. The waitresses working there were just like your grandma; they wore red and white checkered aprons over white uniforms. They loved our crew until? ... Let me ask you how in the world we could get kicked out of a place like the Chicken Pie Shop? Well, we sure as hell did. Kelly managed to find one of those aprons just like the ladies in the restaurant wore, with one very notable exception. We headed for lunch one day and Kelly was wearing his apron. The ladies in the restaurant were tickled pink and formed a circle around him. He showed off the pockets and how cute it was. Remember? I mentioned the noticeable difference? That difference was ... hidden in one of the pockets was a very large knitted "male" digit that would put "John the Wad Holmes" to shame. Kelly waited until all eyes were upon him and whipped out his pride and joy. That's how we got kicked out of the Chicken Pie Shop on a sunny San Diego day.

CHAPTER NINE
Greetings

The job was going well, but I had to leave. Dale drove me to the San Diego Airport for a flight to Los Angeles.

It was 1965 and I'd already received my draft notice and on April 7th I reported to the "Armed Forces Induction Center" in Downtown Los Angeles to spend the next two years in the "United States Army." Working for Bud had one huge advantage. The drill instructors had nothing on him.

While in the Army it was time for my initiation into Local 18. Obviously, I was unable to attend due to my current employment with the Department of Defense in South East Asia. "If he's not present, keep him out," was the call from the old drunks in the back of the hall. You know the ones; after a lengthy presentation by the Union Officer's, they would wake up and say, "I didn't get that, could you go over it again?" They had just spent the last hour listening to the officer lecturing on some subject. Why in the hell would those drunks want to delay our union meeting when we could be done with it and sitting in the Oaks Bar, our usual after-meeting hangout?

The Business Manager, John, echoed their demands not just because of me, he didn't even know me. John had a long ongoing beef with my father, and for a damn good reason. Dad had always seen him for what he really was, a hard drinker with a face like a bulldog chewing a wasp. He spent his working day's "doinking" his secretary and destroying his liver. The secretary, by the way, had used the union credit card to put tires on her boyfriend's car and who knew what else she used it for. John's relationship with the secretary finally came to a head during a union meeting held a year later. John took the stand and with his gruff, three-pack a day, whiskey-induced voice, stated ... "Hear there's a rumor going 'round I'm screwing Eve!" The response from the gallery wasn't quite what he expected. Rather than, "Oh, no, not you, John" ... snickers, elbow jabs and backslaps held forth. You really fooled us on this one, John. Don't get me wrong, I've been a dyed-in-the-wool union member for over 40 years. It's the drunken philanderers like John who give our great union a bad name. Well, anyway back to my initiation; I had a lot of friends in the hall that night, and they put John and his cronies down quicker than he could snuff out a Camel.

CHAPTER TEN
Back in the Good Old USA

I was released from the Army on April 6th, 1967; two weeks later I reported to 1316 Glendale Boulevard to go back to work for Haughton.

The first job was the new Greyhound Bus Depot in Downtown LA. We had two escalators to install. The Foreman was an old timer, "Phil." Phil was Haughton's escalator guy. My Mechanic, Ed, had worked for all the companies. Ed was a good Mechanic and we got along fine with one exception. I was wearing my Army field jacket which still had my Sergeant stripes on the sleeves. He was a little pissed about this and asked me, on numerous occasions, to take them off. I never asked him why, but guessed I outranked him in his earlier life. We set and aligned the trusses and setup the trees with the lines. Ed's toolbox was a mess and being the thoughtful grunt I was, I put it back in good order. The first thing Ed did was to dump the hand tray into the bottom of his toolbox. Then he sent me on a mission to gather all the banding iron I could find. He loved that stuff and would get real excited when I brought him several sizes. From then on he was "Banding

Iron Ed." We worked the job for several months and then pulled off.

The Company sent me down to Korea Town to help on a six-stop geared duplex. It was the usual job with the exception of the guys I was working with. Mike and Ernie (the guys who joked around about taking out "Big Bill's Old Lady) were two bachelors going through their divorces. They had this bachelor pad down in Bellflower. You'd think they had it made. Even with all the booze, broads and Rock-n-Roll, it just wasn't happening. These poor, lonesome guys only got laid on their birthdays if lucky when married and even less as single. "Wild and Crazy Guy ... I don't think so. Boy, these guys were a great team; funny, hardworking and the best practical jokers ever.

Mike, Ernie and I moved over to a new job in Santa Ana. Big Bill was the Foreman and a good one at that. He was 6'4" and as strong as an ox and as gullible as they come. Bill had an old black ford pickup that was his pride and joy. He babied that old truck like it was brand new. I will call Mike and Ernie "The Boys" from now on.

Well anyway, one morning after Bill parked his baby and went onto the jobsite, The Boys started pouring Haughton #32 Motor Bearing Oil directly under the crankcase breather pipe of Bill's truck to form a pool. Every night when Bill left the job site he would "Pre Flight" his rig. Immediately, he spotted the pool of oil underneath his truck. The next morning when Bill arrived at the shack, looking like he just lost his best friend, he expressed his grave concern about his baby. The Boys kept it up for the next few days, increasing the amount each day. Believe me, Bill was a wreck. On Friday The Boys abstained from their prank. On Monday morning Bill arrived at the shack and announced he almost got rid of his baby but the leak had mysteriously stopped. We all looked at each other and never said a word.

Another colorful Mechanic, Charlie, was also on the job. What made it interesting was his personal life. His relationships were always a little on the explosive side. For some reason he always seemed to hook up with women who were either wrestlers or roller derby queens.

Charlie always won the Monday morning story contest on the larger jobs. With several crews working the same job, the stories could and did become very entertaining.

Charlie and his current girlfriend lived on the second floor of an apartment building that surrounded the pool. Occasionally, during one of their serious domestic disputes, the pool ended up as the repository for their personal possessions.

One evening one of the girlfriend's former boyfriends made the mistake of stopping by without calling first. Needless to say, Charlie wasn't all that happy about this unexpected visitor and let him know by knocking him down the stairs. The guy ended up in a heap at the bottom. Charlie figured the guy hadn't learned his lesson, so he tossed him into the pool.

This unexpected visitor became one of the better Monday morning stories.

The argument started with the small and easy-to-carry personal items, such as clothing, going over the rail into the pool. As things progressed, consecutive objects would increase in monetary and then on to sentimental value. While the easily-removed items headed toward the bottom of the pool, the disagreement moved on to small kitchen appliances, TVs, record players, radios, stereo amplifiers along with their speakers. After about five minutes there was nothing left in the apartment smaller than the living room couch or the refrigerator.

The exhausted couple, not to mention, the soon-to-be-evicted couple made up and headed for Sears to replace the drowned furniture and small appliances.

Shortly after finding a new apartment on the "first floor" and furnishing it with their new stuff, things changed and Charlie was sent to Albuquerque. Haughton had a large job over there. This assignment, for all intents and purposes, ended their relationship.

Charlie had to make his escape to Albuquerque, so he figured he would get a U-Haul trailer, load up all his new stuff and get out of town. The girlfriend had to be out of their new first-floor apartment so he could pull it off.

The time came when she took off to visit a relative. It was late and he had to get to Albuquerque. All the U-Haul places were closed. Closed or not, there were plenty of trailers parked on the lot. Charlie had to move fast, so he backed his truck up to a trailer that looked as if it would hold all his stuff. The rub here was the trailer hadn't been checked out for its next trip. Spare tire, maybe? It didn't matter; he hooked it up and headed over to the apartment. After loading all his stuff, it was off to Albuquerque via "The Mother Road," Route 66.

The trip was going great until 200 hundred miles outside of Albuquerque when the trailer blew a tire with no spare onboard. Charlie was a pretty resourceful guy, not to mention a little bit of a gambler. Why not call U-Haul and see if they will come out and fix the tire? They did ... and it was on to Albuquerque. Charlie settled in Albuquerque. He then, in the middle of the night, returned the trailer to the closest U-Haul rental facility. This became the first "Monday Morning Story" in New Mexico.

Mike left the Santa Ana job to go work for another Mechanic named Bill. Nobody liked this guy and Helpers hated working with him. Bill was a genuine prick with lousy work habits to boot. Lousy habit number one ... he threw tools when pissed off. Lousy habit number two ... he had the dropsy's; he couldn't hang on to any tool while working in the hoist way. As the work progressed up the hoist way, more tools hit the pit. His Helper spent more time running down the stairs, jumping in the pit and retrieving tools than he did actually using them. After numerous trips to the pit, this whole deal got a little old for Mike. Finally, Mike decided this would be his last eight-floor roundtrip. He returned with the dropped tool, stepped on the skip and carefully replaced the tool in Bill's hand tray. Mike smiled at Bill, picked up the hand tray and dumped all the tools down the hatch. Still smiling, with a parting shot he said to Bill, "F... you asshole, I'm going to the shop." The last time Mike saw Bill, he was sputtering to himself while gathering up all his tools down in the pit. This was the last time the two worked together.

Ernie went on to become the Business Manager for local 18 and after many years is now happily retired. Unfortunately, Mike passed away a few years ago. He was a good friend and I miss him.

I worked a job with Bill in Santa Barbara for a couple of months and got along with him just fine. This sounds good from the outside but believe me there was fallout. It was a liability to be friends with Bill because every other elevator man in the business couldn't stand the guy. The following is an example.

While working a large job in LA with six other crews, Bill stopped by to pick up a Company tool. Upon his arrival, there were no handshakes, backslaps, jokes or "how's the family" exchanges with anyone except me. This may not sound like much of a problem, but believe me, it could turn into a curse.

If you're an asshole in the eyes of the guys you work with or around, then your friend fits the same category, kinda like "A Bird of a Feather" type of deal. The minute Bill left, the catcalls, kissing-ass gestures and the bending over and spreading of cheeks began.

I had a problem that needed defusing. This unsolicited relationship could haunt me for the remainder of my elevator career. Confronting the other guys with palms up and the best hang dog look I could muster, I blurted out, "I can't help it if Bill likes me!" When they all started laughing, I knew I had dodged this one.

CHAPTER ELEVEN
San Diego Again

Haughton had another big job starting in San Diego. I was on Bud's list, so down Interstate 5 it was.

San Diego Gas and Electric (SDG&E) was the same as all the big jobs I've worked. There were eight 800 FPM gearless passenger cars that served 28 floors and a 500 FPM gearless freight that serviced 30 floors. The material arrived as usual, in and on trucks. We unloaded barrel after barrel of rail brackets and truckload after truckload of rails. The manpower was normal for San Diego. There was an equal mix of locals and LA guys. One of the new hires was Eddie. We called him "Fast Eddie." He was a former New York bartender, easy going and fun to work with. Eddie had never done work like this before. Unloading brackets from the barrels and spotting them at each floor was tough on the hands. Being "Macho Dudes," we didn't use gloves (hand shoes) in those days. Poor Eddie's handle was changed to "Hands." The poor guy's mitts looked like hamburger meat in a few days. Bud took pity on him and gave him lighter work to do until his hands toughened up.

Another new local hire was Larry. Larry was a big, personable guy who had a problem ... he was afraid of heights ... he was "deathly" afraid of heights. Hell, we all were, but Larry was a little over the top. Larry was no quitter and found ways around his phobia. The fire proofers had gotten ahead of us and had sprayed their snot all over the beams in the hoist way. Larry's job was to bend over the open hoist way and scrape off the fireproofing from the beams any way he could. He found a piece of metal lath just the right length. Being the clever guy he was, he found pipe chases that ran through the concrete right next to the hoist ways. Using his custom tool he could reach through these holes and scrape off the fireproofing without even getting near the open shaft. Larry did well in the business and went on to be an ace employee with US Elevator. I ran into him a few years later and he made it very clear that he was one of the best hands US Elevator had. At US they called him "Twinky" because he was a big guy.

Another member of our crew was Justin. He reminded us all of a Kangaroo Rat. It must have been the eyes. Justin was deeply religious but it sure didn't stop him from participating in after-work beers with the rest of us. He was a little nervous and flighty. His religious background came forth when he was driving a 5/8 inch concrete anchor with a very large Roto Hammer while singing "Take a Closer Walk with Thee." Justin was a veteran of WWII. As a combat infantryman, he marched his butt all over Europe. I worked with Justin installing counter weight rail brackets for the big freight car. Using a framing square, we transferred the line to the steel, deducted the distance from the line to the holes in the rail bracket and marked it on the steel beam. Next was to level the marks, drill 5/8 inch clearance holes and bolt the whole deal up. After the bracket was bolted up, we faced the rail surface with what we called monkey balls. Monkey balls were a simple device consisting of a length of string with two 5/8 inch nuts tied on each end. We put the monkey balls across the bracket to square the whole deal up. Simple enough, right? First off, you have to have all the tools. I told Justin that Bud was watching us so we needed to get going and hang this bracket. I asked him where the framing square was and he replied … "I dropped it." "Okay, we can use the level." "I dropped that too," he said. We were 15 floors up with Bud breathing down our necks when Justin hit the stairs to get his tools with Bud in hot pursuit. Justin found his tools in the pit. Unfortunately, they didn't fare well after a fifteen-floor fall. With Bud watching, Justin climbed up on the targets to retrieve his stuff.

I have to stop here and talk about targets. On a big job the targets secure the piano wire that dictates the final location of the guiderails. These things are the heart of the entire job and once set, don't touch them … don't even "breath" around them. The whole installation is based on their integrity. Never step on them even if your life depends on it. Justin not only stepped on them, he ran all the way across the other targets to find out what Bud was trying to tell him. He found out all right …"Get off the "F---ing" targets, Justin."

There was a short story in my career that could have had two endings. If it weren't for Kelly, it would have ended in the worst of the two possible scenarios. Kelly and I were realigning the targets for the counterweight rails at the end of travel on the 30th floor. We had a bridge plank across the hoist way. I stepped off the steel onto the plank to move the counterweight target, missed my mark and fell through the space alongside the plank. We had the skip tied off two floors below and that was it. There was nothing but air on all sides. I hit the beam in the back of the hoist way one floor below. I managed to grab that beam on the way down and landed on my right side. I was hanging on for life and drifting in and out of consciousness from the pain. Kelly slid down a main guiderail to where I was hanging on, grabbed me in a bear hug and held me up against the beam and told me a joke until I regained consciousness laughing. Kelly saved my life. There was nothing between "me and my Maker" but Kelly.

It was time to install machine beams and the derrick landed 5,000 pounds of 16x8 inch beams on the steel at the penthouse level. Kelly and I measured the distances between the building beams and using a cutting torch, we cut the new machine beams to fit inside the web of the building steel. Then we welded a short piece of angle on each end of each machine beam. The angle extended beyond the length of the machine beam. This piece of angle allowed us to drop the new beams in between the building steel at the proper height and also allowed us to move them around to drill the holes and set them up per the layout.

Each elevator required three beams. That added up to 24 beams total, not including the service car. Now the fun begins ... we had two-blocked the skips which gave us a platform to work from. Bud had ordered up a magnetic drill motor but it was on another job. We used our big B&D industrial drill motor equipped with an "old man." An "old man" was a piece of pipe and a chain with a cargo hook attached to the end. The pipe had a notch in the end of it. A link of chain would fit in the notch. The cargo hook was attached to the work which gave us pushing power at the other end of the pipe. Each beam required twenty-eight 7/8 inch body fit holes. Kelly and I would get together to push on the drill motor to get through ½ to ¾ inch steel. The unpleasant part of this work was the blue hot-spring-shaped shavings that came out of the hole. These shavings always found their way into our shirts via our open collars. We figured out later that rags used as bandanas would prevent a great deal of pain and disfigurement. Well, Kelly and I had a pact. Whoever stopped first because of the pain prior to completion of the hole was deemed a pussy and responsible for the first beer and pool game that afternoon. This bet was concurrent, meaning you could be buying all night. Haughton used 7/8 inch insertion bolts for attachment; these bolts had spiral rows of teeth rather than a shoulder. One guy was on one side with a single jack (sledge hammer) and the other guy was on the other side cranking them down with a ¾ inch ratchet. When the whole deal was bolted together we torqued the bolts down to about nine zillion foot pounds. We had finished two hoist ways when a new magnetic drill motor arrived just in time to handover to a different crew, so we could start with the rest of the machine beams. Then we could begin drilling sixteen 7/8 inch holes in the bottom of the beams. And then we could hoist and bolt up the 1,200 pound double-wrap deflector sheaves. These holes had to be drilled directly into the overhead and those blue hot-spring-shaped shavings had a direct shot at our bare skin. Same bet as before except this job was more painful, so we doubled the beer/pool bet.

Little Dickie's dad was a longtime Haughton Mechanic and a damn good one at that. As it goes in the business, his son followed in his footsteps. The difference between Little Dick and his dad is Little Dick was a whole lot funnier and had more balls than "The Barbers Cat." One day at SDG&E he went down in the annals of elevator history. Bud, as usual, went about his pusher duties like a bear with a serious case of hemorrhoids. He was always serious, tough and grumpy with no nonsense tolerated. Little Dick was assigned the exciting job of unpacking wooden crates that contained fixtures. The crates were right next to our shack for two reasons. First we could keep an eye on them and secondly they were a great place to plant your butt during lunch. Little Dick tackled his assignment with enthusiasm. He was so enthusiastic that he was finishing up before Bud returned with his next assignment. Being the good Helper he was, he stayed busy. To fill in his time he went into the shack and toe-nailed four sixteen-penny nails into the lid of Bud's pride and joy, his old wooden gang box. He built it himself and it had followed him for years from job to job and state to state. Little Dick not only had the balls to nail Bud's box shut tighter than a Pharaoh's tomb but he waited for Bud to return to the shack and asked if he could have a handsaw to help with opening crates. Bud, in his usual tough-guy manner, unlocked the lock, pulled on the hasp and bingo ... he almost pulled his arm off. This is impossible, so he yanked on the hasp with even more effort. A dark, menacing look came over his face with the recognition that somebody, yes somebody had seriously messed with him. "This is not a 'F---ing joke;' this is destruction of private property and I'm calling the cops." Little Dick, with his testosterone on mute, in a solemn concerned voice said, "Who could have done a crappy thing like that, Bud." Shaking his head Bud replied ... "I just don't know, I just don't know." For years to follow Bud blamed me for this prank, and it wasn't until years after Little Dick left the business and Bud and I became good friends that I ratted out the true culprit.

During our lunch break at a gin mill across the street from the job, Little Dickey was the man of the day. This dive had great Polish Sausage sandwiches and when consumed, masked the beer breath acquired during three games of pool and three quick beers. Dick passed on the sandwiches because he couldn't stand the smell of horseradish. His aversion was so ingrained he couldn't even stand to be near anyone who had a Polish Sausage sandwich for lunch.

We, unlike the so called hardhats of today, removed our hardhats when not working. Enter Kelly ... we distracted Dickey long enough for Kelly to rub horseradish on the inside of the sweatband of Dickey's brain bucket. All afternoon it was, "Get away from me you guys, you smell like that horseradish crap." He finally got the picture when he arrived home and still smelled like a Polish Sausage sandwich with horseradish.

Bud picked up another Helper, Jimmy or JD as we called him. JD was a great kid, personable as hell, easy to laugh, hardworking and just fun to be around. He had been with us awhile and felt comfortable enough to share his personal life ... Big Mistake. Doing so with this bunch is like jumping in the shark tank at Sea World with a nosebleed.

After informing us he was newly married, he went on to share some details of his love life. (A note here ... elevator guys did talk about their personal lives but bedroom details with wives, was off limits, unless they brought it up themselves.) I said wives; girlfriends, on the other hand, were open season. The details he shared with us indicated some coaching might be in order. Doug, another new Helper who had been married several times and now a bachelor with a very active trap line of young women, looked like a good candidate for JD's pep talk. After spending some time with Doug, JD remarked, "At quitting time I'm gonna go home and try that." The next morning in the shack, prior to starting time, we all couldn't wait for JD to walk through the door. A new JD was among us, ear to ear grin and a face that looked like he'd been trying to teach an in-heat 400 pound lioness to use the cat box. In years to come JD and I worked together and became the best of friends.

George was an LA Mechanic who joined our ranks three months into the job. George was about 6'3" and had one of those mouths that dropped at the corners. Early in his elevator career a coworker took a look at him and said. "With your mouth looking like that, you remind me of those big-ass Wally-eyed Catfish, we used to catch as kids," hence, the handle "Catfish."

George had a lot of trouble managing his personnel life, like child support for former and present wives, kids and even support for ex-wives' boyfriends. With all these responsibilities, George was not a happy man. As a matter of fact, at the jobsite he was like a bear with a sore dick. Being pissed off all the time made George a hard guy to work with. The best way to get along with him was to ask his advice regarding relationships. He was kind of a Dr.

Laura with balls. If you kept the questions coming, he kept occupied with giving advice based on his own personal relationships. The thing is, the answer was always the same. When asked a question he would get out his marker, draw two squares, point at them and say, "This is black and that is white." In a nutshell, that is the way his life was organized.

One day while getting off the skip his head intercepted a bucket full of miscellaneous nuts, bolts and anything to add weight. The Iron heads had suspended this 30-pound bucket using piano wire as a giant plumb bob to align some work they were doing. Being Iron heads, they neglected to attach a safety line. A torch they were using cut the piano wire and down it went center, punching George directly in the center of his hardhat. The impact drove his head right down into his shoulders. Six-foot-three George was now six-foot-one George. Being the tough guy he was, he just kept working.

His personnel life was catching up with him and the Marshal's were visiting the jobsite weekly. They would ask if there was a "George" working here and we would say, "Never heard of him." The last time I saw him, he was coming down a stairwell when an ascending Marshal passed him hot on his trail. Story goes, he joined some religious cult in Oklahoma and was never seen or heard from again.

It was hotter than hell up on top of the SDG&E building with the sun reflecting off all that bare steel. The contractor supplied water coolers with ice at all the landings next to the outside construction elevator. One particularly hot day, Kelly brought in packets of pre-sweetened Kool Aid and dumped the contents into the water jug. It all started out to be just for us and the Iron heads because we were, for the most part, the only guys up there. Word got out and soon the outside elevator was filled to capacity with guys riding up to use the rent-a-can and quench their thirst at the same time. The contractor got wind of our miniature refreshment station and reacted the only way he could, he got pissed off. First off, the Iron head boss was interrogated; no result there. "What the hell do you mean my crew put Kool Aid in the water jug … you have to be kidding." We were the only ones left and due to our less-than-stellar track record with the contractor, the blame trickled down to our benevolent Foreman, Bud. Just two days earlier Kelly, with a three-foot pipe wrench on one shoulder and a thirty-pound hand tray full of tools, staged a "trip" and recovered his balance like a high-wire act right in front of the GC while walking across a six inch beam thirty floors up in the air. Bud was on the hook and what else could he do? Yeah, you got it, get pissed off. The next morning in the shack, "I know you guys did it," staring at Kelly and me, "But I can't prove it." End of story this time.

We were having our share of accidents, nothing major, just stitches, bruises and stuff like that. Because SDG&E was one of the larger jobs going for Haughton at the time, we were the squeaky wheel.

One day Bud trotted out this guy from the insurance company who was equipped with a clipboard, a pocket full of pens and pencils nicely encased in a "Bozo" pocket protector. He couldn't have come at a better time.

We were building car frames in one of the banks of four elevators. The building floors were poured but the walls were not up. With this stage of building construction it was easy to see what was going on. Bud and the insurance guy took up a vantage point on an open stairwell adjacent to the four open hoist ways where we were working.

Little did the insurance guy know that as the day unfolded, he would witness a scene that would go down in insurance-man's history. My guess is, that day is still being talked about at meetings, over coffee, during sex, while enjoying martinis and may even be included in instructional manuals. And here's how it went.

My duties that day were to serve as a Helper's Helper. The Helper I was helping was named Jim. Jim was a senior Helper and Bud's right hand man.

The story begins with a bang. Jim had bent over to tie his shoe or something when I walked past him carrying a 3/8 inch drill motor with its cord dangling behind me. Right in full view of the insurance guy and Bud the cord swung around and hit Jim in the eye. Jim's first reaction was to check out who was watching and after spotting Bud and the insurance guy dropped to his knees with his hand covering his eye. He put on such a great act we didn't know whether to call an ophthalmologist, the ambulance or the coroner. This Pratt fall couldn't have been better, at that point the insurance guy whipped out one of his "Cross" pens and began writing like mad on his clipboard. Little did he know he would get writers' cramp times ten today. Jim staggered to his feet and, with my assistance, we slowly disappeared from sight.

From their vantage point Bud and the insurance guy were able to watch the crews building car frames. After the insurance guy re-holstered his Cross pen in its Bozo pocket protector with its company logo on it is when Kelly came on the scene.

Kelly was coming down the open stairwell on the opposite side of Bud and his observer. He saw an opportunity to further his legend. Kelly shouted down to Vince to throw him a single-jack. Vince picked up the hammer and during his backswing, the insurance guy ran out of ink in Cross pen number two i.e., during the forward motion of Vince's arm, Cross pen number two ran out of ammo. As the hammer left his hand the insurance guy, like a well-trained infantryman, grabbed his trusty BIC backup and continued writing without a hitch. During the hammer's upward trajectory, BIC number one gave up the ghost. As the hammer impacted Kelly's mouth he frantically reached for BIC number two. When Kelly fell backwards covering his mouth, BIC number two ran out of ink. He was completely out of writing utensils when Kelly crawled up the stairwell as if mortally wounded. All the guy could do was to stand there wringing his hands.

What this guy didn't know was he had just witnessed one of the best acts in elevator man history. In the shack the next morning we all expected the other shoe to drop . . . Bud didn't say a word.

As the job progressed Kelly continued to entertain us; you never knew what to expect. One day he jumped on the skip with me and had sawed half way through his hardhat with a hacksaw leaving the blade in the hardhat without its frame. Another day he showed up with half his goatee shaved off. He also had a brown leather cowboy belt that was a little too long. He cut off the end of the belt, colored it red, stuck it in his mouth and wandered the jobsite with this four-inch tongue hanging out.

Kelly was very good at math; the "water drop" was a prime example of his skill. He placed himself several floors above his intended victim with a hardhat full of water. Next he would plot his victim's escape route, pour out a small amount of water directly over his victim and then pour the rest of the water where he had calculated the victim would be during his escape. Using this method, the water didn't just hit the victim on the top of the head. The victim, while escaping, ran into a wall of water because of Kelly's very precise calculations.

Kelly and I laid out the machine room equipment. The other crews set the machines and welded them down. Kelly told Bud he wanted to go back to LA because he missed his kids. He had five boys and one girl. Kelly went home and that was the last time I ever saw him. Some years later I was working back in LA and heard he was over in Las Vegas working for the big "O" (Otis Elevator) with a full leg cast on his left leg. The story goes, he got in a fight and the other guy broke Kelly's leg. Otis had him wiring controllers and selectors so the cast was no big deal. Years later out of curiosity, I called the LA Local from San Diego for some other business and happened to mention Kelly. They informed me there was an inquiry about him from a shipyard up in the Pacific Northwest. It would be years until I heard about him again.

Over the years, I would hear little bits and pieces about Kelly. I was working in Seattle when I ran into an Otis route man who had a story about someone I might have known. This guy was working on an elevator in a dam in Eastern Washington. One of the guys who worked there told him about a colorful, short little Irishman who came out to do some work on their elevator. This guy arrives at the dam with a little travel trailer in tow, checks in with the maintenance guys and gets setup with a parking space right next to the river. He checked out the elevator and the material that had previously been shipped to the site. The job entailed replacement of the door locks and fixtures. He asked the maintenance guy how the fishing had been lately and what they were hitting. The maintenance guy informed him it was great; Skagit spinners would do the trick. After hearing that, the elevator man informed the maintenance guy that the new door locks which the Company had sent were the wrong Hertz. He said he had called the Company, ordered the right material and it would be delivered to the dam within the week. The maintenance guy had been around the block and thought the story a little odd, and that it had a slight smell of BS, but just maybe there's some extra magical stuff when it came to elevators and he bought the story. The elevator guy headed for his trailer grabbed his fishing gear and was only seen occasionally for the next week. After listening to the Otis guy's tale and description of this mystery elevator Mechanic, I knew this had to be Kelly.

Vince affectionately known as "Winnie the Ginny" was the most typical New York Italian I've ever had the pleasure of knowing. He was short, handsome with black hair parted in the middle with big feet that didn't fit his small frame. Vince got his name from one of his Helpers "Freddie the Alien." Freddie was from Germany and had trouble pronouncing his Vs. They came out as Ws, thus the name Wince.

Vince was a high-strung Mechanic who always stayed busy. Some Helpers had a problem with the fact that Vince always liked to finish what they were doing, even if it took until 7 p.m. ... two and a half hours past quitting time. Vince was working at SDG&E and had an encounter with one of the different people we meet in our trade.

Buck was a tower crane operator of questionable gender. He was a big guy with an unusual build. He always wore dark glasses to hide his drinking habit that extended into working hours. The most unusual trait was his bra. Most of the construction guys steered clear of him simply because he was very volatile and an asshole to boot.

I was working for Vince and waiting for the man lift at starting time when the incident occurred. Vince had never met Buck before and thought the bra was some kind of joke. Vince proceeded to approach Buck from behind, reach under his arms, grab his chest with both hands and say "Oh, I like these." Buck exploded, turned red and grabbed Vince by the shirt, picked him up and said, "If you ever do that again, I'll kill you."

I was working as Vince's Helper and according to the Helper code you would give your life if necessary in his defense. Being devoted to my Mechanic and, not to mention, liking the guy, I started looking for a weapon. Someone had left a long-handled shovel next to the entrance of the man lift. I picked up the shovel and assumed the Babe Ruth position and yelled, "Let him go, you son-of-a-bitch." This got his attention and when I caught his eye, he knew I wasn't kidding; he gently set Vince back down on his feet.

A few years later I heard that Buck, while shitfaced as usual, dropped a yard of concrete on a guy while he was working a bridge job. The guy was killed. Maybe I should have taken that swing after all. Someone might still be alive today. "Who Knows?"

Vince didn't look for trouble, but it usually found him. He had a bit of a temper and it didn't take much for a minor incident to turn into WWIII.

After Kelly left, Vince became first Mechanic and ran all the machine room work. The laborers drug a leaking hose through the machine room and it was spraying water all over our equipment. Vince exploded and grabbed the hose and started pulling it out of our area. The problem was, on the other end of the hose was Frank, the labor Foreman. Frank was the spitting image of Vince in size and temperament except maybe his shoe size was smaller. Each potential combatant was pulling on the hose and moving toward each other at an alarming pace. With the "Clash of the Titans" just seconds away, some type of action had to be taken to prevent serious injury to one or both. Jumping in between them would be like jumping in between two speeding freight trains heading toward each other on the same track. A fight would have been bad enough but we were 30 floors off the ground with nothing but air around us. Yelling at Albert, a laborer friend of mine, to get in front of Frank, I then got into the fray by jumping in front of Vince.

The four of us became squeezed together like sardines in a can. All of a sudden, there was silence and then, thankfully, there was laughter along with handshakes and backslaps … just another day.

Like all jobs, SDG&E was winding down. I was able to run a car for the contractor for a few months and that was it. Haughton had nothing coming up in San Diego. I could return to LA and work for them or take my chances on the bench in San Diego.

CHAPTER TWELVE
San Diego for Good

It wasn't long before I was able to get on with Montgomery. Montgomery had purchased a large independent called Elser. Family owned and the largest independent elevator company in the area, they had been installing their junk in San Diego for years. Did I say junk? I really mean junk. Their stuff was awful. The good side of this is, it broke down a lot and created tons of hours for their employees. The only parts they bought from Montgomery were parts they couldn't cobble up in their shop. They built a hydro valve nicknamed the "Bear Trap." They also built a selector that didn't move up or down side to side or back and forth; it coiled up. This thing came to be known, not affectionately I might add, as "The Cobra." When Montgomery took over, the infrastructure remained pretty much the same. Family members and friends of family members provided the labor force for Montgomery in San Diego.

My Mechanic at Montgomery Elevator Company (MECO) was Frank. We called him "Mumbles" because of his duel hearing aids which were the result of the big guns on the ships he served on during WWII. The hearing aids allowed him to hear himself in a low tone but, unfortunately, no one else could hear what he was saying. I found out early in the game how important it was to understand what Frank was saying.

MECO was installing a lot of hydros in San Diego at the time so they had about five crews doing nothing but that. We were one of the hydro crews. The equipment they were installing was not Montgomery, but US. Somehow they thought by buying a US package, sticking a MAC operator on it and making good time in the install, seemed like a good idea.

The way it worked was … a US truck would stop just short of the job site, place a Montgomery magnet sign over the US sign and drive on in to deliver the material. It usually worked until one time when the driver, while in a hurry, put the Montgomery sign on upside down.

Back to understanding Mumbles; we hoisted the rails into the hoist way using a single whip. I was on one floor and Frank was on the other. With the rail hanging in midair, Frank mumbled something; I said, "Okay" and was promptly pulled into the hoist way still hanging on to the rope with the rail attached. My upward assent stopped when the rail hit the pit. What Frank mumbled was, "I have a rope splinter in my hand so hang on so I can pull it out." From that point on I always made sure I knew exactly what Frank was saying.

Frank and I worked together for quite awhile and became very good friends. Frank was one of the luckiest guys I ever knew. The Shell coin game was in progress and every time he filled up his old blue international, he won something. Another time, while walking onto a jobsite, we both spotted a wad of bills lying on the ground. Frank grabbed it first and counted out $38. "Frank, that's great; that means $19 for you and $19 for me." "No, that means $36 for me and a beer for you." I did get that beer and a few more to boot. With his luck still holding, he found $200 in fifties next to a deflector sheave in a secondary space at the Naval Hospital.

Frank's good luck became bad luck when it came to his domestic life. His wife was a shrew and pretty much ruled the roost. She was tough and tried to keep Frank in line. Frank had it worked out though. Coming home late, he didn't even have to enter the house for a good night's sleep. He carried an electric blanket in his truck. When arriving late he would sack out on the recliner on the front porch, plug his electric blanket into the porch light and off to Never-Never Land.

It can get cold in San Diego during the winter and on one near-freezing night just after Frank dozed off it got very, very cold. The wife had figured out Frank's climate control system was dependent on the porch light switch. Turning off the switch and bolting the door drove Frank's comfort level to that of bunking outside in Antarctica. Frank spent that night in the backseat of his International.

Frank was a handsome guy and women loved him, but he was a straight arrow. We were adding a landing to a vault elevator in a bank downtown when a doll, and I mean a doll, took an interest in him. She knew what she wanted and asked him what he did for fun when not installing elevators? Not quite fed up with his home life, his answer was, "Well, the family keeps me pretty busy."

On that job the building had installed plywood partitions to separate our work area from their office space on the landing we were adding. Being good elevator men, we checked out the office behind the partition and noticed a very nice looking woman working at her desk which was up against the partition. After eyeballing the layout, we took some measurements on our side and drilled a small hole. The test hole was off by about four inches and displayed a knee. Another hole displayed what we were looking for and it provided a welcome visual relief from the rigors of elevator installation. There was a problem; the air conditioning in the office where our target of interest was working blew a stream of cold air through the hole we had drilled. This stream of air hit us directly in the eye, so after a few minutes of viewing, we had to change eyes, but still we would develop a rare syndrome known as "Phenomena of the Eyeball." The syndrome progressed to a point where when the boss showed up and looked at us, he asked, "You guys been drinking? Your eyes are bloodshot as hell!" "Well, no," was our reply, and we had to share our little peep show. Shortly after, we sealed up the hole with duct tape to remove the temptation. I have to admit the tape was removed and re-taped on at least one occasion.

About a year later Frank was on his way out of his marriage. Another fox, who happened to be his neighbor, recognized his potential and was able to keep him pretty busy. Last I heard, he was doing great with this gal and living happily ever after.

Most of the hands at MECO San Diego were holdovers from the Elser days. These guys had never worked for anybody else. When work was slow the nonworking guys would show up at the shop in the morning in hopes that a job would come up. With this readymade labor force hanging around in the parking lot, the Company could man jobs as they came up. As far as the Union was concerned this deal wasn't all that Kosher. The Local couldn't do much about it and the Company didn't have to pay anyone show-up time.

The Elser-Montgomery men were a pretty tight bunch and as stated above, they had spent most of their working careers with the same Company. In order to stay in touch in the San Diego area, they all installed CB radios in their vehicles. One might think this type of communication would aid in getting the work done. Not so, the real purpose was to find out ... where is coffee, where is lunch, where are we meeting for after-work beers and most importantly to stay one step ahead of the boss, who just happened to be a "dickhead."

The boss was the son-in-law of the former owner and had a last name that actually rhymed with "Lick-a-Dick" which became his handle over the radio waves. He may have been a dickhead but one thing for sure, he wasn't stupid. Stashed away, out of sight, in his office was his own CB radio that just happened to be tuned into the same channel his employees were using. These guys were busted big time and the boss cracked down hard on them. He started checking and double checking hours, whereabouts and quitting time. It took awhile for the guys to figure out their code had been broken. Once done, they became the hardest working elevator men in San Diego and Lick-a-Dick became "Mr." on Channel 11 but still remained Lick-a-Dick on the newer sideband radios he couldn't monitor on his older radio.

Frank and I continued to install these counterfeit Montgomery-US elevators. Montgomery had around five crews installing this equipment and tracked the installation time on a large chart in the boss's office. According to the progress chart, Frank and I were always just behind the rest of the pack. Over a beer one afternoon, we figured out why we looked as bad as we did. The chart was set up with seven categories; unload and store, jack, rails/car frame, entrances/doors, cab/wiring and adjust. It was simple; the categories we excelled at were missing. If the boss would just add coffee breaks, lunch and picking up, we were sure we would be able to catch up with the rest of the crews. As mentioned earlier, the other guys were family or friends of family. I found out later just how strong these family ties were when Frank suggested they put me up as a temporary Mechanic when they had more work than they could handle at their current manpower levels. Their reply was, we have to take care of family first, and they did just that by giving a tough job to a son-in-law. The kid was as green as they come and managed to botch the job badly. It wasn't his fault. It took another crew quite awhile to get the job right.

I was trying to get ahead and the future at Montgomery looked pretty bleak when you had to get in line behind guys who couldn't even come close to you in the experience department. The ranking system was based on a family tree rather than experience and knowhow. The whole thing wasn't much of a deal, just normal small company stuff.

My boots had all the hydro oil they could soak up and the work outlook was bleak at Elser-Montgomery due to the politics. I missed the bigger jobs so it was time to move on to greener pastures.

The Business Associate (BA) called and said Westinghouse was starting a big job in Downtown San Diego. They heard about me and needed an experienced card Helper to work their job. I answered the call and went over to the contractor's shack and met Andy, the Foreman. He was kind of a legend in the trade, especially on Westinghouse (WECO) equipment. He'd been around for quite awhile, knew his stuff and ran a safe job; we hit it off. Along with Andy was Ray who was a little older than Andy and had the same qualifications and was the first Mechanic. Ray would leave to start his own job down the street in a couple of months. These guys had a little game they played with the card Helpers, "a chance to turn out." They went to each card Helper and said, "We're going to need another Mechanic and we've been watching you." The conversation ended with, "Don't tell the other guys, okay."

Turning out as a Mechanic is one of the biggest deals that can happen to a Helper. Hearing that, I put in a triple effort and took on work that perhaps I shouldn't have. It turns out they gave all the card Helpers the same line, so they could get some entertainment watching the interaction among the card Helpers … a shitty little game. After we all found out what was going on, we (the braver ones) vowed to even the score. First off was Andy who came to work dressed as if he were on a golf outing. The only thing that set him apart from Arnold Palmer was his Westinghouse blue hardhat and the Wellington work boots. Being the best dressed man on the job made him a perfect target for handfuls of wet, sloppy fireproofing. Lessons from Kelly's water drop technique came in very handy, by the way. There were days when Andy left the job looking like "Frosty the Snowman." The last and best is when we found a piece of Styrofoam and shaved it down to the same size as a full counterweight filler and then painted it "Westinghouse Grey." The real thing would weigh in at around 170 pounds. Approaching Andy with strained faces, one on each end of this bogus hernia-maker, we said, "Andy, help us with this." His reply was less than helpful. We got right in front of him and used the two-tie rod holes we had drilled like a Norton Bombsight. We targeted his non-steel-toed Wellingtons and yelled "Watch out!" Then, we dropped it. During its descent, his eyes got so large you could see them bulge out from under the brim of his hardhat.

Union Bank had nine gearless DMR cars and one hydro. I looked forward to working on equipment other than Haughton. It didn't take long to figure out Westinghouse had it together. Haughton was still having growing pains with their traction products, while on the other hand, WECO had it pretty well figured out and just kept on making a good product better. Hell,

WECO even got away from that old elevator green to a nice easy-on-the-eyes grey.

My job with Andy was to be timekeeper, safetyman and Union Steward. When I wasn't doing that, I ran the catheads, hustled rails, wired, installed fixtures and just helped out where needed until the machine room equipment was set. There were some other perks; guys with whom I'd worked at SDG&E, Doug, Twinkie and JD were also on the job.

After the rails and platforms were installed, I moved on to the machine room crew. WECO had a guy, Bob, aka, "Bobby Joe Dingle Finger" who was their wiring Guru.

Bobby was this cool hillbilly who knew his stuff. His job was to setup all the wiring tables and to preflight the controllers. The latter was quite a job because WECO soldered everything. All soldered connections had to be checked and then re-soldered, if necessary, before field wiring commenced. He was quite a guy and came equipped with an old stainless steel thermos that never left his side; it had a capacity of about two gallons. A steel handle was attached to the thermos via copper pipe strapping and was fastened with #10 machine screws and nuts. Full load weight was in the neighborhood of about seven pounds, and it never seemed to be empty.

The metal coffee cup that accompanied the thermos hadn't been washed for some time so the original color was unknown. Its capacity was probably about half a gallon unwashed, but to find out the actual capacity of the cup, we decided to clean it with solvent, you know, the same stuff we used to clean rails. The capacity went up about 25%. Note here: We performed this test without Bobby's knowledge.

Bobby matched his thermos and cup with his rolling stock. He drove a war surplus Power Wagon. This vehicle wasn't your everyday Dodge Power Wagon. It also wasn't just a plain ole US WWII surplus Power Wagon. This was probably a Soviet Union surplus wagon originally sent to the USSR via Lend Lease and returned to the US. You know, kind of like they did with Russian war brides.

Early on I realized how different WECO was from Haughton when a truck full of rails pulled up to the job. I figured a few Helpers would unload the truck like they did at Haughton. Not so, everyone pitched in and got the job done. Second time was when I was hustling rails and running the catheads. All of the Mechanics in the hoist ways had all the rails they needed, the top row of rails had been cleaned, so I picked up a broom and started cleaning up. Ray walked by and said, "Sit your ass down and take a break; you're not working for Haughton now." Another noticeable difference was when a truckload of elevator equipment showed up at the jobsite and the whole crew unloaded it rather than leaving it to the two greenest Helpers.

I liked Westinghouse and thought there might be a future with them. They had a service department in San Diego that might provide a steady job and definitely provide better working conditions than construction.

We saved all the scrap wire and sold it so we could have a party at job's end. It was a nice shindig at an equally nice restaurant. All was going well and everyone was having a good time until the woman I was with became very volatile. She was a bartender and had been around the block, twice or, maybe even, three times. As a matter of fact, she was famous for actually throwing two junior Naval Officers out onto the street while working in a beer joint on El Cajon Boulevard. Hanging out with her was like being a member of a tag team in the WWF. The night was still young when she got into a beef with "John the Dutchman's" ole lady. This wasn't hard to do as John and his wife could be very confrontational at times. Nobody on the job liked John. He was a very good Mechanic but he was just hard to get along with. John was usually the last to be hired and the first to be laid off. Work was slow in San Diego and he hired on with a company in LA. He got a report date and hopped on the Grey Dog late in the evening and headed for LA. Around 11 p.m., after getting off the bus, he called his new employer and told him to come and pick him up. It's not hard to guess what happened next. By the end of the phone conversation, his one-way ticket became a roundtrip ticket back to San Diego.

Back to the party . . . there had been some preliminary blows struck between the women, nothing serious. John stepped in between my date and his wife and apparently there was some form of body contact between John and my date. She looked at me and said, "You hit him!" I did and Ray jumped in my face and shouted, "You stop right now." He was much bigger than I and also a Foreman, and it was time for us to go.

That right cross pretty well ended any chance of a future with Westinghouse.

CHAPTER THIRTEEN
Back in the Fold

The "Elevator Gods" smiled again when Haughton started a nice traction job in Santa Ana. I got the call and was soon working with "Big Bill" as his Helper. I was also the Union Steward and Safety Man. Just like the old days, Bill was his usual self and great to work for. I ran rails, catheads and filled in where needed. It was a great job and I got to know Bill very well.

The daily drive back and forth from Santa Ana to San Diego was a hassle but well worth it because I was back working with my friends and to top it off, Haughton had booked a large four-car gearless job in Escondido that would start in the near future. The job went smoothly and when Bob joined us, it made the workdays even better. Soon we had all the cars running on temporary and ready to adjust.

Palomar Hospital in Escondido was a great job. We had four gearless ten-stop elevators to install. Even better, the job paid subsistence and was only 40 minutes from my house and it was a reverse commute to boot. There was Ernie, Jerry and best of all, Uncle John. It was a great crew.

Ernie was a great guy with whom I had worked in the early days. Jerry was not only a great Mechanic but a topnotch Adjuster as well. Jerry had a gift; he remembered anything and everything he ever read. He had come up through the ranks and during that journey he had worked with my Father and soaked up all the knowledge Dad had to offer.

The job consisted of a three-car group of passenger cars and a single-service car around the corner. We started out with building targets and dropping lines, washing and running rails and building our skips.

John was his usual self and a lot of fun to work for. He would entertain us during coffee and lunch by reading porn magazines to us. One time he was so engrossed in the story he was reading that his cigarette burned all the way to his fingers; he didn't even flinch.

I was John's Helper and had to stick pretty close to him because he never filled me in on what was next. He told me that if I was a good Helper, I needed to anticipate his every move. I learned this the hard way when I stopped to use the "Rent a Can." It took me a half an hour to catch up with him on the tenth-floor landing. From that point on I took care of personal matters either during coffee break or at lunchtime. John didn't have much in the way of tools and the tools he had, he guarded with a vengeance and expected me to do likewise. An example was when a laborer grabbed John's tin snips from a pile of doors and left the jobsite for good. John started his detective work and after a few inquiries we identified the culprit and it was off to the Laborers Union Hall to retrieve his tin snips. He spoke to the union rep about the larcenous laborer and was informed the stolen tin snips would be back at the jobsite shortly.

Once you left the jobsite with John for any reason, the way back was never a direct one. There was always a bar on the way. Two hours later when back on the job, Jerry and Ernie informed John his tin snips had been returned to their original location with a thousand apologies.

John knew how to get along with the General Contractor (GC) and especially the crane operators. His secret was a bottle of VO. The GC always appreciated it and it made life easier for us. The bottle that went to the crane operator guaranteed the use of the crane during its free time without being charged for crane time like the other trades. On the other hand, when we had skips in the hoist way and a running platform, John's law was that they ran on VO. Most of the trades that needed access to the hoist ways presented gifts of VO to John. Kind of like when the Three Kings showed up during the birth of Christ.

One trade refused to bring a gift to Uncle John ... the lathers. They figured they could use our skips when we weren't, like during coffee or lunch. These guys would watch us like a hawk and the minute we disappeared, they sprang into action, jumped on our skips, worked as fast as hell and returned everything to normal before we got back. This worked for these guys for awhile until they decided to take a break themselves and left all of their tools and material on one of our skips. John shows up out of the blue and throws all their stuff down the hatch. Well, these guys certainly learned their lesson and a bottle of VO was presented to John within minutes.

Working these jobs was a dangerous deal, and you never knew when an ugly accident would happen. We were waiting for the man lift and we heard a loud "thump." When we looked over we saw a man lying in the construction debris that always surrounds these jobs. We ran to him while one of the other trades went to get help. The man was a cement finisher who was sacking the poured concrete columns up on the sixth floor when he lost his footing. When we got to him, he was alive but in horrible condition. He had several broken bones protruding through his pants. We told him that help was on the way. All he could say was, "please help me" and we comforted him as best we could. This building was an addition to the existing hospital so the Aid Car was there in minutes and the Medics took over. It was back to work. Later in the day we heard he didn't make it. Out of respect, the job was shut down for the day and it was a sad day for all.

As stated earlier, John loved his beer and wasn't bashful about sharing his passion. By about Wednesday, if John said, "Is it time?" and plunked down some green, the ritual began and all work was finished for the day. Ernie and I would walk over to the liquor store and bring back a case of Bud. We did this every Wednesday and Thursday. Most days the first case didn't last until quitting time, so the ritual would repeat itself. Our shack soon became the gathering spot for the other trades. I can't believe we were able to jump into our cars and drive home after six or ten brews. Fortunately there were no accidents or brushes with the law.

The job wound down so John and Ernie pulled off and returned to LA. This left Jerry and me to do the adjusting and to sell the job to the customer and the State Inspector. Working with Jerry was a blast and the day consisted of adjusting elevators, getting lunch from McDonalds and ending the day with Buds in the cab of his truck.

The last time I saw Dirty John was when I stopped by his home in Azusa. I had been sent to Los Angeles by US to survey a large mod they were bidding on. John was getting close to retirement and slowing down a bit. His body may have been slowing down but his brain kept him going as the same old "Dirty John." Did I say "Dirty John," well not quite. There had been a change in John and based on what I witnessed during my visit, "Farmer John," might now fit the bill.

John opened the front door and greeted me like a long-lost friend which, of course, I was. After the backslaps and hugs, we settled down at the kitchen table to shoot the breeze over a couple of beers.

It was a warm day and the slider to the backyard was wide open and after the second beer I felt an unusual presence, not to mention, an all-too-familiar odor that didn't belong in the kitchen.

Hearing a loud snort, I looked over my shoulder and there stood a full grown brown-eyed, pink-nosed, brown and white cow. John noticed the shocked look on my face and said, "Guess you want to know about Emily here?" "You bet," I said.

John went on to tell of bringing home a calf that was supposed to be raised up and turned into steaks, ribs, roasts and hamburger. However, the only thing this calf was turned into was "Emily." The first mistake John and clan made, was to name her. Emily progressed from a farm animal to a family pet or perhaps to a family member.

I asked John, "Does Emily have a cat or maybe like a cow box?" "Nah," was his answer and further explanation revealed that the sliding door was only open after Emily had finished all her business in the backyard. Emily's visits were limited to a few minutes during each day or on special occasions such as birthdays, Thanksgiving, Christmas or my visit.

John passed away just when he was starting to enjoy his retirement out on the blue waters of Lake Mead.

After-work beers with my buddies from LA were common. This was not always appreciated by the woman I was living with. "Honey, I'm home," began with planting my butt in my favorite chair. The first hint of her displeasure was the double-decker tuna sandwich whizzing by my ear, ricocheting off that favorite chair, impacting a newly painted wall and sliding down that wall to come to rest on the brand new carpet. It was time to beat feet before she could do bodily harm to my person.

With Tijuana just a few miles away, it was an easy destination for blowing off steam. Hitting the main drag, Avenida de Revolution, the Chicago Club was a sure bet for some entertainment. It was downstairs with a large dance floor, plenty of "B" girls and a bunch of Sailors and Marines to make the evening interesting. And believe me, they did. I found an empty chair and asked four of our finest fighting men if I could join them. I was welcomed with handshakes and backslaps after informing them I was a veteran. It was the same deal in all these joints, "B" girls hustling drinks and dancers on the floor collecting US legal tender for a face rub in intimate places.

After a couple of Dos Equis, it was time for a pit stop. Upon entering the bathroom, I was immediately confronted by this little guy pushing me around and shouting, "A dime to pee." Being in no mood for this, I proceeded to grab him by his shirt and stuff his head in the galvanized trough that served as a urinal. He then started calling for a guy named Victor. Victor hit the scene and let me tell you, this guy would block out the sun if he was outside. By that time I was realizing how stupid I was. I pulled the little guy out of the urinal, wiped him off completely and gave him two bucks. Victor was another matter, the ransom was five bucks and I paid it gladly.

I went back to my seat by the dance floor with my newfound GI friends who were way drunker than when I had left them. It was the same deal; the dancing girl would approach a fighting man, accept the half dollar that was offered up, grab the back of his head and pull it into a perfumed crotch. While the GI was thinking he was getting his money's worth, the dancer would grab his beer bottle and stuff it into the other side of her anatomy. After that the dancer would move on and the GI would take a swig from his beer bottle which now had a new and unusual taste. I decided to fill this guy in on what had just happened. Needless to say, the GI was very pissed off and wanted revenge. A plan was hatched.

The GI would take a near-empty beer bottle and heat the top with a Zippo lighter. Note here, every GI has a Zippo lighter with the wick pulled way out. The resulting flame would match that of an M132 Flamethrower. Now that the top of the bottle was as hot as the Zippo could make it, the GI waved his half dollar around as if he was trolling for tuna. The girl who took the bait was the same one who pulled the beer bottle prank earlier in the evening. After setting all this in motion it was time to get the hell out of there. As I ascended the stairs that led to the street, the red-hot beer bottle top found its target and the place went nuts. I could hear the yelling, scrambling and furniture rearrangement. It was good to be out of there and heading home. I hoped the tuna sandwich was cleaned up and all was forgiven.

I was in my car and on my way to the Good Ole USA with my driving somewhat impaired by the numerous Dos Equis I had consumed. Another guy and I attempted to share the same lane. There was an impact; he made his escape and I found myself lit up by flashing red lights. I pulled over and the motorcycle cop requested my keys. I complied and sat down on the curb. Minutes later a black squad car arrived with two very big and very serious looking cops in black uniforms. I found out later that these guys were Federal Cops and it would be unadvisable to mess with them. They started pushing me around and I managed to get one good punch in and that was it. You know the sound that's made when you thump your index finger on a half empty carton of milk? Well, that's the same sound I heard as these guys were thumping my gourd with their rubber clubs. It took about three or four blows before I became as gentle as a two month old kitten. They cuffed me and pushed me in the backseat of their car. By this time I realized just how much trouble I was in. Hey stupid, you just hit a Mexican Federal Cop. This could lead to a stint in La Mesa State Prison and a leading role in "Locked Up Abroad." What became the saving grace was that the same woman who pitched that double-decker tuna sandwich had connections. She had worked with a guy named Bustamante on a project to publish a Mexican phonebook. In other words, this phonebook was published in the US, distributed in Mexico, advertising US businesses such as tractor dealers, etc. Bustamante was also the publisher of the "Noticia," the largest newspaper in Baja, California. This guy had a lot of juice in this neck of the woods. In an effort to minimize my upcoming punishment, I deeply apologized for my previous behavior and mentioned Bustamante was a friend of my family. There was some chatter between my two captors and they stopped the car and asked me to get out. Oh shit, did this mean more thumps on my already-bulging skull? Or, will this be my mysterious disappearance. I could see the headlines ... "Stupid Gringo Missing in Mexico." To my relief, the cuffs came off and we got back into the squad car.

The trip to the Tijuana Jail was uneventful. Upon arriving we entered the building and I was asked to take a seat in an office. The new cop behind the desk was cool and told me I could smoke if I wished. There was some amount of paperwork and I was then led out of the office into the cellblock. The jail itself was a two-story affair and my new home would be on the first floor. I was working a large job at the time and I was tight with all the other trades.

While passing through the cell block I heard, "Hey, Jim" around five times. It seemed half the guys I was working with were sharing the same fate as I.

After being locked in my cell I checked out the accommodations. There were four bunks, two on each wall and a toilet on the back wall between them. My only cell mate was this hippy guy with shoulder-length hair. I asked him how he got there; he told me they picked him up because of his hair. Note, these were the late 60s and Mexican cops were known to arrest guys just for having long hair. All was quiet and I crawled up on one of the upper bunks and tried to sleep it off.

I was suddenly awakened by a combination of factors. With my body in the first stage of a 9.0 hangover, it was going to take awhile for my fogged-up brain to process just what was going on. First, there was a body next to mine in the bunk; this body happened to belong to a very large pissed off black guy. Second, we were not alone; there were ten other guys sharing the same cell along with my newfound "Bunkie." Third, half of these guys were trying to crawl into our bunk. The fog had cleared somewhat and I was able to figure out what was causing all this pandemonium.

Over the course of the evening, the cell had filled up with guys who were beaten up, drunk and whatever. As the cell filled with bodies, the toilet filled with barf, blood and crap. In order for this place to keep its four-star rating, the guards would wash out each cell every morning with a fire hose. They not only washed the floor they washed out the toilet as well. The stream of water splashed its contents all over the cell. The safest and cleanest place was the upper bunks. The cleaning crew and their fire hose had moved down the line leaving us to our own devices.

As the morning passed, our cell's population dwindled until it was my turn. I was herded out of the cellblock to an office door that had been cut in half. Behind that half door was a judge. He looked at his paperwork and told me it would cost seventy-five US dollars to get out of this place. I told him I didn't have the money; he said, "Okay fine, you can make a phone call." I called Frank (Mumbles) and he told me that he would be happy to come and spring me, right after he put his washing machine back together. "Hey, I'm at Devil's Island for Christ's sake; can't you get down here any sooner?" Being very "Pussy Whipped," his answer was "No!"

A guard took me to a different cell up on the second tier. My new home had three other guys in it so each one had their own bunk. It took some time to get to know the other guys and I found out all but one were GIs. The non-GI had been in there for seven days and had seven days to go. I didn't dare ask him what he was in for … serial killer, maybe. Shortly after my arrival, a Navy Chief came to the cell door with a guard. He asked if there were any Military personnel in the cell. Three answered in the affirmative and were let out of the cell on their way to freedom along with an Article 15.

Checking my surroundings, I noticed a cell that was downstairs full of women and guys too! The cell was really two cells with the middle wall knocked out. There were blankets hung up for privacy. We couldn't get over the fact that guys were sharing a cell with the women. I asked a passing guard what the deal was. He, in the best English he could muster said, "You know, they gay boys." Got it, they put the gays in with the women so there won't be problems with the other male inmates.

A guard came and got me; we went downstairs and there was Frank with a large grin on his face. "I wish I had my camera." He paid my bail and we took off. The first stop was the Old Heidelberg for a few beers and food. He dropped me off at the impound lot, I paid the fees for my car and headed for home. When I got home the mood was cool but manageable.

I had a passenger, a little passenger, a little illegal alien passenger that crossed the border with me. This little bug would make commando raids in certain private places and attack my mid section with vigor. He would wait until I was sitting down watching TV with beer in hand and then he would strike. Yes, and strike he did; this little bugger had a bite that hurt like hell and raised a red welt the size of a quarter. I tried everything I could to get rid of him short of the time-tested crab-removal tactics. Tactic one, shave your privates, pour lighter fluid on the unshaven side, light it on fire and stab him with an ice pick as he flees the fire. The other method, tactic two, would only work if there were two or more invaders. Pour bourbon on your privates, wait ten minutes, sprinkle salt on the area. If the Bourbon got them drunk enough they will kill each other in a rock fight. In a few days my little passenger had split. While thinking back on this, I was very lucky indeed. La Mesa prison is where I could have ended up due to my stupid behavior. It makes for a great story though.

CHAPTER FOURTEEN
A Grunt No More

Orv was a longtime Haughton employee from the Upper Midwest. He'd been with the Company so long he was probably Nathaniel Haughton's first Helper. Nathaniel founded Haughton some 100 years ago. You never saw Orv without donning a suit or a sports coat. He loved to drink coffee and eat soft ice cream while talking about the "good old days" back in the Midwest. He talked about when he worked on freight elevators which Haughton had installed in the Rust Belt.

Orv was the typical died-in-the-wool company man. He had been running the San Diego office since Haughton had purchased EMCO. To call him a fiscal conservative would be an understatement. Orv wouldn't pay a dime to watch a piss ant eat a bale of hay. He employed his wife, whom we called "Mom," on a part time basis to do payroll and the other paperwork that a four-route branch generated. "Mom" received minimum wage and no benefits.

Orv had an ongoing grudge match with the LA office. He had a large sign in the office which read, "We Don't Give a Damn How They Do Things in LA."

Our San Diego office consisted of a storefront with a backroom on the first floor of a fleabag hotel south of Broadway. On occasion, so many drunks and down-and-outers would pile up in our doorway that the cops had to scoop them all up and haul them off so the office could open in the morning.

We had quite a bit of work in San Diego. Haughton had just shipped a Model I Electronic Velocity Control (EVC). It was a pretty good piece of gear, but like all new products, it had its problems. I installed, adjusted and turned over quite a few of these elevators. I owe it to Orv who first turned me out as a Mechanic and later as an Adjuster. The only reasons I became an Adjuster was first, I had been an Adjuster's Helper for the last two years, second, I could read the manual, third and foremost, Orv wanted his own Adjuster so LA wouldn't interfere with his operation by sending a guy into his territory. Being on my own with only the manuals to refer to put me in way over my head and it probably took years to correct some of my mistakes. Fortunately, as my knowledge increased, I got to the point where I knew what I did wrong and could cover my past screw ups.

Orv's visits to our jobsites were pretty typical. He'd walk into the machine room unannounced and after greetings all around, he would start his ritual. The ritual was pretty much the same from job to job. He would assume the position with his hands behind his back and his head bent forward somewhat like Groucho Marx. If he encountered a small piece of hardware he would pick it up and look at it as if he'd just found a prize. He would then hand this prize to me and proceed to lecture me on its cost. The cost-effectiveness lecture on this piece of hardware could continue for up to ten minutes. When finished, he would hand it to me and ask that I find a safe place for it.

If we had cars in service, he would move on to the running machines. During his past visits we learned that one man had to be stationed by the disconnect with one hand on the switch already exerting ten pounds of pressure just in case Orv's tie wound onto the brake drum just like a Penn 500 Jig Master Fishing Reel. It was pretty damn scary watching your boss lean into a running geared machine with his tie flapping on the rotating brake drum.

The 101-day strike was just around the corner when I was sent to Los Angeles to help adjust a large mod at LA County General Hospital. I'd been on the job for a week when we stopped work so it was time to head back to San Diego.

Orv was all set for his "Golden Years;" ready to pack up and get out of town and bingo! ... We went on strike. He had to stay in his little place with no furniture until we all went back to work.

A couple of weeks into the strike I got thrown into the briar patch. I found a job on a sport fishing boat which was pretty cool. All I had to do was walk down to the pier and get on the boat. I worked the deck and cooked. The job didn't pay all that well but it was a lot of fun anyway. Halfway through the strike Oliver & Williams who had signed an interim agreement picked me up because they needed a card Mechanic. Jim, the guy I was to work with, was a temporary Mechanic so basically I took his job. There were some hard feelings to begin with but we managed to work it out and spent the next three or four weeks installing hydraulics all over San Diego. It was a lot of fun and Jim was a great guy to work with. Unfortunately, a year later Jim had a serious accident and was killed while installing a duplex in Pacific Beach. He and his Helper had secured a skip and went home. They came to work the next day, got on the skip, and it fell. They had made a serious mistake because they did not secure the skip to a rail bracket and just depended on the skip's safeties to keep the skip in place. The skip started down the hoist way and after several floors into its descent, the skip's safety rollers burned out. The skip then fell all the way to the pit. Both men were seriously injured. Jim passed away in a few days and Kenny was out of work for about a year.

It's hard to see friends die like that; an accident that really shouldn't have happened.

The strike was over and Haughton had booked a nice little job that involved the tear out of an Otis external-geared freight and the installation of an ESCO Hydro with power freight doors. This job had a great advantage because after landing the car and counter weights, we used the old machine as a hoist. We wrapped the governor rope around the driver a couple of times, lowered it down the hoist way and hooked up a pendant station to the existing controller. We then had a readymade hoist for removing the old equipment and installing the new.

Ernie, our Superintendent, was running us out of LA. He had been my Dad's boss years before. My Dad is mentioned in Chapter One, "The First Elevator Man I Ever Knew." Ernie was the same petty, pain-in-the-ass guy with whom Dad had worked those many years before.

This job ponied-up a lot of scrap. We used the proceeds to purchase tools that we couldn't get from Ernie. This was normally accepted by the Company. All was good until he spotted a load of scrap in my truck. "I want the cash from that scrap," he said. I tried to explain what we were doing, but he wouldn't hear of it. Having no way out, on the way home that night I sold the scrap for around fifty bucks. On my time ticket for that week I entered $50 for cartage. Over the next few weeks he got his cash and I got my cartage.

The next bug up his ass was, "You can't pick up your checks at the shop on payday; it's a waste of time, so give me an address where you want your checks to be mailed." What he didn't know was while we picked up our checks at the shop, we also dropped off our time, ordered parts and picked up or dropped off tools and material. I gave him the address where I wanted my check mailed … 312 Cushman Place. It worked out just fine. We were still able to drop off our time, order parts and pick up or drop off tools and material as 312 Cushman Place was "The Shop."

John was our new Branch Manager right out of Toledo. He was Buckeye to the bone, a nice guy but a little flighty. The service guys had nicknamed him, "Gunther" and it seemed to fit very well. He was new to fieldwork and dropped by our jobs quite often. We'd have lunch and discuss the current job we were working. My Helper Jimmy, while kidding around, came up with a great gag. Jimmy and I rehearsed this gag for about a week and it was time to spring it on John. John showed up on one of his noontime visits as usual, and it was off to Denny's. Very casually, I mentioned that we needed a week off. John, being the nice, casual guy he was, swallowed his food and after some time asked, "Why?" "We have to go to Milwaukee," I answered. Another mouthful disappeared. "Why?" John asked. It was time to spring the trap. Taking a deep breath I answered, "Jimmy and I have been selected by our Local to participate in "The Elevator Man's Construction Derby." Two mouthfuls of food went down this time. John, with a puzzled look, asked, "What's that?" Here's where the rehearsals paid off. "Every five years the International holds a competition where we stack rails, build car frames, install cabs, wire, you know the whole works. We compete with guys from locals all over the country." Four mouthfuls hit bottom before his face lit up and he exclaimed, "I'm really proud of you guys," and when I get back to the office I'm calling Dick! Dick was the Regional Manager. Mission accomplished! After lunch Jimmy and I looked at each other and said, "Is it time yet?" Well, we really liked John so we made the call to tell John that he'd been had just about the time we figured he would hit the office. He wasn't very happy and wouldn't even trust us for "good morning" for the next two months.

If ever a crew was tight, it was Harold and Al. These guys were so tight they took vacations together. The heavy of the team was Harold. He was a "BSer" beyond compare. Al, on the other hand, was the straight man of the two. Harold would fill our heads with BS all day long. You know, sexual exploits, super Mechanic war stories and fantastic elevator installations. After digesting all of Harold's banter, we could always rely on Al to give us the "real story." This came in handy when it was time to trip-up Harold. When we got to Harold, he would start to stutter and re-tell the story a little closer to the truth. This was a little game we played all

162

day. The truth be known, Harold was a hell of a wrench, excellent pilot and an all around good guy.

These guys were also pranksters and not too bad at it. One of their tricks was to tape up the inside lens of a welding hood with duct tape and ask you to weld, while all the time saying, "You're a better welder than I, so will you weld this joint for me." Not bad and somewhat entertaining but most certainly Bush League. Harold and Al always laughed their butts off and were proud as hell of themselves. Payback came when they returned from one of their joined-at-the-hip vacations.

Harold had an old sheet metal hand tray he built himself and it was his "Pride and Joy." He painted it Haughton green using one of the spray cans the Company shipped with every job. It was winter and pretty cold in the shack so we would fire up the Babbitt pot for a little warmth and heat up a sandwich or two. There were blocks of Babbitt in the corner and it didn't take long to come up with a plan. Ten pounds in the Babbitt pot, heat until molten, remove Harold's tools from the hand tray, pour molten Babbitt in the bottom, let cool, spray paint with Haughton green, throw some dirt in, replace the hand tools, put back in the job box and finally, anxiously await Harold and Al's return from their vacation.

Day one, Al opened the job box and grabbed the hand tray and it was off to work. Quitting time was just the opposite. This went on for at least a week and we wondered if they were on to us. Finally, they came into the shack at quitting time and Harold said, "Al, why don't you take some of those damn heavy tools out of that tray?" With every eye glued on Al, he complied, dumped the tray's contents on the concrete floor and found himself still holding an empty hand tray that weighed about 15 pounds. "Some jerk poured Babbitt in the bottom of this damn tray!" he exclaimed. There were some feeble attempts at reprisals but still there was no question that the rest of us had the upper hand in the "Gotcha" game. The work picture remained good for the next year. Finally, the well went dry and it was off to LA.

I was sent to State College in Alhambra, which just happened to be the place where I grew up. This job was a six-car group with a service car in the back. By this time Haughton had worked out most of the bugs on their "Works in a Drawer." My Helper on this installation was "Little John." Little John's dad just happened to be "Uncle John" whom I had worked for in the past, so we had a lot in common. This kid was probably the best looking guy around. It was almost embarrassing to be around him because of all the women who were all over him all the time. We were able to get the job finished and work was picking up in San Diego so we parted company. Last I heard, he had left the elevator business and was running a marina at Lake Mead. Talk about a kid in a candy store.

Back to San Diego and back with John (the guy we tricked with the "Elevator Construction Derby" ploy). John was one hell of a salesman and he proved it when the State outlawed tiller-line elevators. There were so many of these that the local companies got together to divvy up the spoils. John would attend these meetings, take everything in and run out and underbid the other guys. This made him pretty unpopular in San Diego but a real hero in Toledo. We converted so many of these things I can't even remember how many. It was great work and to make it even better, I had another great Helper . . . Jimmy. Jimmy was a young guy who would laugh at anything and when he laughed he showed the pinkest gums you ever did see. He was an accomplished welder and fabricator which came in very handy. We were more like plumbers and pipefitters in those days. I found out he is now happily retired after doing repair for US for years and years.

The first conversion John booked was a sidewalk elevator right on Broadway in Downtown San Diego. Being our first, it became very obvious there was going to be a lot to learn. This elevator was just a plain old tiller-line that ran from the basement up to the street level. It had no wainscot or sidewalk screens to keep the public from falling down on the platform when the car was at the lower level. John misread the new code and sold them sidewalk gates. We fabricated new screens right on the spot and welded their hinges to the metal parameter that had been set in the concrete sidewalk. We fabricated new wainscot with sheet metal and angle iron along with an expanded metal swing door in the basement complete with an interlock. We cobbled up a little controller that would operate the ECCO down-valve that replaced the three-way valve. The three-way valve was operated by the tiller-line. A check valve was also installed so the car could run up on the pump. A plug for the pendant station on a cord that had constant pressure up-and-down buttons was installed in a hole that was cut in the sidewalk door. A stop switch was mounted on the wainscot and this elevator was ready to see the light of day again. The premier was scheduled for the next morning. Those in attendance were, The State Elevator Inspector, the building owner, John, Jimmy and me. We had caught the attention of about 15 pedestrians who were held up at the "Don't Walk" light. The gallery wouldn't be disappointed! Jimmy was in charge of the pendant station that contained the up-and-down buttons. "Let her rip," I said, and a chain of events unfolded with amazing speed. The car came up like the first stage of an Atlas rocket at the Cape. Jimmy stood there in shock and didn't let go of the up-button as the car proceeded to rip off the gates, pull the steel parameter out of the sidewalk and finally came to rest on the stop ring four feet above the sidewalk. The whole thing sounded like a garbage truck dumping the contents of a dumpster in its hopper. Jimmy looked at me and said, "That's what the long toe guard and extra steel on the bottom of the car is all about." In the past the car could run above the sidewalk and unload stuff off the back of a truck. At that point the car failed inspection and the inspector, John, the building owner and 15 pedestrians backed away with the same dejected look they would have if the San Diego Chargers had just lost the Super Bowl in the final seconds of the game. We did finish the job after learning gates weren't required if the car could only be controlled from the pendant station at the sidewalk level. We welded a new stop ring on the jack to limit the over travel to six inches. We adjusted the hoist way switches so they would actually stop the car. Because we did all this work on an unpaid holiday right in the middle of Downtown San Diego, you guessed it ... one of our brothers called the hall. We had all that fun but after the fine we didn't even get paid.

John continued to sell tiller-line conversions and most were sidewalk elevators. Those warm, sunny days provided leg shots galore when we worked on the platform with the sidewalk at eye level.

John moved on to greener pastures and hired on with US which took him to a job on the East Coast. His replacement was a longtime Haughton employee who had been running the Haughton office in Portland. His Portland trap line had been getting shorter and shorter until the Company finally figured out they didn't need a Branch Manager anymore. After all those years with the Company they handed him his walking papers. The Elevator Gods smiled upon him and due to his relationship with Dick, who was the Regional Manager, it was off to sunny San Diego.

John's replacement had arrived. Russ had worked for the Company forever. He was a WWII Vet and served in the United States Navy. He spent most of his time at sea and was aboard one of the ships that picked up survivors from the USS Indianapolis.

Russ started out by telephoning all of us and introducing himself prior to a face-to-face meeting. After a week or two he covered all the bases by visiting all of our major contracts. Slowly, our customers started asking us, "What's with this guy?" "What do you mean?" we would ask, and their answer was, "He smells like a gin mill." Russ had a little problem. We figured his drinking caused him to lose his job in Portland. San Diego was probably his last chance. All in all, Russ was a pretty good guy, but his drinking was getting to our customers. In spite of this problem, the work was out there. Russ was a good estimator and pulled down a bunch of work due to the State of California requiring the first version of fire service. Our larger customers signed on the dotted line at the get go. This meant there would be a ton of work for me. The first go around on this new code was to add an early form of Phase One. The elevators that were affected by these were usually service cars. In other words, the State wanted one car in the building available for Fire Department use during a fire emergency.

This was great work, inside, in an occupied building with lots of pretty girls. Toledo did the engineering, marked up the wiring diagrams, rounded up the material and sent the whole deal out to us. My Helper during all of this was Tommy, aka, "Engine Tommy." This guy was a whiz at rebuilding engines and he even rebuilt a Ford 302 that powered my fishing boat. Tommy was a blast to work with. He had a great sense of humor and every day we had a new laugh. Boy, this guy was cheap though. The question of the day was always, "Can I have that?" He'd lug anything and everything home every night. He was a great looking kid and the women were all over him; this became a serious problem. Case in point ... we always had morning coffee at a greasy spoon in Downtown San Diego. There was a good looking gal who also had her coffee at the same time we did. The minute she laid eyes on him she became a "Tommy Stalker" and she, not only made his life miserable but she could have shortened his life expectancy due to the fact that she was married to this huge San Diego Cop. The situation became so serious we finally had to pull up stakes and find another place for our morning caffeine fix.

We had just completed Phase One recall on the service car at First National Bank, and it was back in service and running fine until ... a few months down the line.

I was on call when an overtime call came in on this very elevator. I checked in with the security guard and went looking for the elevator. The PI lights were out so it was a simple matter of picking a couple of locks to find the car. I picked the lock at the bottom floor and no elevator. I traveled to the top floor, picked that lock and still no elevator. I went to mid travel, picked that lock and still no car. But something else was missing … the comp ropes. I went back to the top floor for another look, picked the lock again and checked out the hoist way. The traveling cables were there okay, but wait a minute … this is the top landing. This time I looked up and there it was, way up in the top of the hoist way. It was time to go to the machine room. I looked down the cable block-out in the machine room floor and two inches below the slab was the two-to-one sheave. By now it was midnight and there was nothing that could be done anyway. I gave the security guard the bad tidings and headed for home.

Because his job was hanging by a thread to begin with, Russ was always acutely aware of his profit and loss statement. Overtime calls on full-maintenance jobs stretched thread a little tighter. So every morning when he hit the office he checked the log for overtime callbacks. If there had been a call you could bet on getting a page at 7:30 a.m. on the dot. The twenty-question routine could get a little irritating before the start of the workday. So with his hand on his wallet the questions would begin. "What happened at First National last night?"

"DC overload was tripped."
"What caused that?"
"The overhead."
"Gasp,"then, "What overhead?"

"The overhead at the top of the hoist way."

"Did you get the car running again?"

"No."

"Why not?"

"It was on the safeties."

"What stopped you from running the car up to release them?"

"The machine beams."

Phone hits carpet . . .

Fumbling noise.

"Where are you?"

"First National."

Dial Tone . . .

Russ didn't show at First National for some time, probably because the gin joint near the shop didn't open until eight.

It was time to check out the damage a little further. I knew the comp ropes were missing so I started at the pit. The comp sheave was lying on its side over in a corner. The comp sheave had safeties so the guiderail-mounting hardware had pulled out of the pit floor. There was a lot of rope piled up in the pit, but not all of it. The ropes were hanging off something up near the top of the hoist way. Picking the lock up on the twentieth floor solved the mystery of why all the comp ropes weren't in the pit. When the comp hitch pulled off the safety plank, somehow one of the ropes looped itself over a leveling vane bracket and after sawing it nearly in half, it hit its center of gravity and slid to a halt.

Tommy and I started the repair by picking locks, pulling out about 20 feet of rope, cutting it off and piling it on a cart. Needless to say, the building occupants were a little concerned about all this chopped up cable lying on a four-wheel dolly. With all the comp rope removed from the hoist way, we had to get the car off the safeties. About this time Russ shows up, looks around, shakes his head and heads back to where he had spent the morning.

There was about four inches of clearance between the car and the overhead so there was enough travel left to get the car off its flex guide safeties. The last landing for the car was a mechanical space that had a 25 foot ceiling. To get into the car we used an extension ladder to get high enough to cut a hole in the wall above the car's entrance.

Backing up here, a few months back we had installed Phase One and Two on the six passenger cars. There was a new console in the lobby for the security guard. The console had the fire service switches along with some security features. The guard who manned this station was, to say the least, overwhelmed by all the switches and lights and he had little or no training.

We had the ladder up and were in the process of cutting a hole in the wall when something caught our eye. There was a smoke detector on the wall just above the elevator entrance. You guessed it … the dust from our excavation activated the sensor right before our eyes.

On Phase One the six passenger cars were sitting at the lobby with the doors open. The guard panicked, hit the evacuation alarm and called the Fire Department. By the time I hit the stairs, making the twenty-five floor descent, all the while squeezing by fleeing building occupants, there were 200 evacuees in front of the building when the San Diego Fire Department pulled up. With a sheepish grin and a turn of the bypass switch, normalcy was resumed and it was back to work.

This time I hijacked one of the passenger cars for our personal use, just in case of another disaster. We could get inside the car and go through the escape hatch to setup our rigging. We setup an A-frame in the machine room and with about ½ inch to spare, hoisted the car off its safeties. From that point on it was a matter of replacing the comp hitch, repairing the pit equipment and replacing the comp ropes. While cleaning down the hoist way, the second smoke detector was activated. This time I was able to get to the security console and prevent the guard from touching anything. The turn of a key switch and a vanishing act prevented another fiasco without anyone even noticing.

We knew what happened, but not why? The car had so much overhead that when it traveled up it didn't break traction. In fact, there was so much overhead that the car traveled right on past the end of the hoist way normal limit cam. The final limit cam mounted on the car ended up above the final limit switch. There it sat, stuck in the overhead, grinding away until finally the DC overload tripped, shutting down the whole deal. By rights the car should have broken traction when the counterweights bottomed out on the buffer. Haughton had had problems in the past with traction and never really addressed the issue. We did install cam extensions and the car was returned to service.

I answered another call on this elevator a few months later. The car was in the upper final limit and stayed there this time. By chance, I started checking the running circuit and felt a faint buzz on one of the relays. There should be no buzz here. This relay had a 220 VDC coil and with the safety circuit open there should be no voltage whatsoever. The meter indicated around 100 VAC. This car was an older Haughton ALNC with 220 VDC running circuit and above ground 208 VAC for most of the other logic. This was a throwback to the "Good Old Exciter" days.

Fortunately, the problem was right in front of me; I just had to find it. I started pulling controller wire and checking the wiring diagram and, lo and behold! ... There was a wire that didn't belong on the DCLB relay. During the fire service upgrade we had added a new wire on top of an old wiring change. This wiring change was buried under a pile of old, black controller wiring. It also wasn't on the as-builts that engineering used to engineer the fire service revisions. This field wiring mistake plugged 100 VAC into the 220 VDC running circuit. This was not enough to energize the 220 DVC running circuit, but under certain conditions, this stray voltage could keep the running circuit powered up when it shouldn't happen at all. This was a wakeup call. It took several months for this problem to show up. All of the above makes you stop and think about all the wiring changes made on dozens of elevators still out there in service. What about that jumper that's missing from your tool box. Anyone who has worked on hundreds of elevators has found that missing jumper left by some other guy; I know I have!

My father was still living at the time and I knew he had adjusted this car initially. When I told him the car disappeared and was lost in the overhead, he laughed and told me he, too, had lost the car during a buffer test. In those days the final and normal limits were disabled and the driver had to slip. Well, it didn't slip for him either. The comp hitch came off and all the rope ended up in the pit.

Unfortunately, about this time, I lost one of the best Helpers I had ever worked with. US had their eyes on Tommy for some time. They made him an offer he couldn't refuse. They put him up as a Mechanic. Tommy remained with US the rest of his elevator career and retired a few years ago.

The State was good to us when they started requiring fire service on most of the elevators in California. The next job was an installation of fire service at the San Diego Gas & Electric Company (SDG&E). This job was one of the Company's anchor jobs. Working this job, for the most part, as a wireman throughout construction gave me an edge for the work to follow. SDG&E had an eight-car group with a large service car. We had all the fire service upgrades down pat. We shut down a car with one guy in the machine room making wiring changes and the other guy installing key switches in the car and lobby. This job did have a couple of hiccups though. The first one came when we had to cut out the marble in the lobby for a Phase One key switch. The marble in the lobby had a beautiful textured finish and had been handpicked in Italy by the marble contractor prior to its installation. There was no way I was going to start punching holes in it. No big deal, get a marble guy to cut the hole. I called the original marble contractor and talked to the owner, Angelo. Now have you ever known a marble guy who wasn't named Angelo? Well anyway, he said he'd send out his best guy the next afternoon. As promised, his best guy showed up on time. This guy was a real marble man. He wore a concrete-spattered hardhat that must have weighed eight pounds. He spoke broken English with an Italian accent. He was also named Angelo and carried a bucket full of rusty tools and was wearing a red 49ers tee-shirt. I showed him the cutout area I had carefully laid out with a black marker. He studied it for a second or two and then, to my surprise, took out a rusty claw hammer and broke a hole through the marble which was twice the size of the hole I'd laid out. "What the hell are you doing?" I yelled. Waving his hands back and forth in Italian speak, he calmly replied, "No worry, no worry." "What do you mean no worry, no worry?" I was already visualizing one or more of SDG&E's VIPs stepping out of one of the elevators and spotting a miniature entrance to "The Carlsbad Cavern." The marble man was right on with, "No worry, no worry." All he did was take all the broken pieces of the Italian marble out to his truck and cut the lines I'd marked. He returned and glued them back in place. The President and CEO of SDG&E couldn't notice the difference if they tried.

Back on track, this one was again going great until the second hiccup. The car station covers were flush-mounted one quarter-inch steel, covered with plastic laminate that matched the cab finish. The laminate had engraved information around the stop switch that became very crucial later in the project. In those days we took the car station covers to San Diego Sheet Metal and they punched the holes for the new switches. At that time there were two new holes because we were also installing a newer style stop that required a larger hole. My Helper who lived near San Diego Sheet Metal would drop off the covers and layout the location on the new holes. He would pick them up on his way to work in the morning. We had seven cars done when he arrived one morning with both covers for the last car. Note: There were two covers per car. While we unwrapped the covers we noticed one very serious screw up; the new holes were punched right in the middle of the engraved text (In Emergency Push Button). While my Helper stood in the corner of the machine room quietly whimpering, it was time to figure out how to get out of this mess. The cover was toast and there was no doubt about it. Hang on here, all we had to do is get new matching plastic laminate (Formica) and get the whole deal to a cabinet shop. They, in turn, would soak the covers in lacquer thinner, remove the old plastic laminate, glue on the new stuff, trim it all up and we could then get them engraved.

First off, we had to get the covers to the plastic laminate store for a color match. They had it all right, but there was one serious rub. The original plastic laminate had a shiny or polished finish. The new stuff was an exact color match but had a matte finish. There was no way we would be able to locate an exact match. Plastic laminate with that color and finish had been discontinued years ago. We went ahead and bought the new plastic laminate, had the cabinet shop do their work, had the sheet metal shop punch new holes (in the right places) and finally we sent it off to the engraver. Now what? ... We had covers that were an exact match for everything except the finish. The guy in the plastic laminate store really saved the day. He suggested we use rubbing compound and try to rub out the finish until it had a polished finish. It would be just like restoring your car's dull or oxidized finish. We started with heavy compound and then worked our way down to the fine compound. After a dozen trips down to the elevator for comparison purposes, we ended up with a perfect match. I left San Diego a few years later and, to this day, I wonder if those car station covers ever returned to their original matte finish on their own. My Helper was sworn to secrecy and moved back to Indiana anyway. Believe me, I never, ever asked my closest friends, who were still servicing that job, about those covers.

San Diego had two full routes and I normally did repair and construction. I only did service work during the other guys' vacations and overtime calls. If you're around long enough, you see a few Branch Managers come and go. There is always the same pattern with the new guy. They run out and sign up customers that nobody else wants. In some cases we had done everything in our power to get rid of these dogs, and if we were lucky enough we did. Here comes Russ. First thing he does is run out and grab these jobs that all the companies had passed around for years. It looks good on paper, until the pigeons come home to roost. I have to say, these jobs did provide a lot of entertainment when it came to trouble calls.

The boss had just booked an old fleabag hotel called "The Californian." There were two elevators, an AC passenger with swing doors and a tiller-line hydro freight in the back. The passenger provided one of the most interesting calls I have ever answered. We'll start with the layout of the lobby.

The lobby of this dump was fairly typical. There was a long couch that normally housed around eight to ten residents in various stages of decay. The couch faced the elevator which was the center of activity for the entire hotel. Upon arriving, I looked into the vision panel and saw that the car was about four feet above the floor with the inner door open. I noticed something else ... legs, long legs, legs that ended at the hemline of a very short red skirt. By this time the guys on the couch had spotted me and were starting to come out of their semi-conscious state. I'll hit the machine room, fix this thing, and get on home. Whoa, not so fast. To get to the machine room you had to walk across the entire roof. There is no way to compare this journey. You had to pass by every vent for every toilet and sink in the building. I've walked by hundreds of sewage vents in my time, but these where different. These vents were almost lethal. There had to be something terribly wrong with either the sewer system or the tenants' digestive systems. It could even be the food served in that area. All I can say is, it was a mad dash with rag in face to the machine room. Once in the machine room, I found the manila governor rope unraveled and wrapped around the governor itself. No fix here, rag in face then mad dash to the stairwell. Back in the lobby it would be an easy deal to get the trapped passengers out. I needed to get a ladder and unbolt the swing door lock. I heard a rustling sound and a kind of low conversation behind me. Looking over my shoulder, I noticed the old timers on the couch had become even more interested in what I was doing. Most had reached full consciousness. I got the swing door open and the legs were still there. To this day I can't figure out how a great pair of legs like that could be somehow attached to one of the worst looking faces in San Diego. With the door wide open and the car at shoulder level, I'd seen all I needed to so it was time to get on with this deal. I put the ladder up against the toe guard and said to the guy in the car, "I'll help you out and you help her out, okay?" He answered in the affirmative. He backed down the ladder and the rustling behind us increased. It was her turn so she started backing down the ladder. At this point it was obvious she didn't believe in underwear. She was backing down the ladder with her partner's assistance when I heard a loud snap behind me. Glancing over my shoulder, I couldn't identify the source of the snap but every eye ball on the couch was not just wide open but beyond wide open. To this day all I can figure out is that while she backed down the ladder, exposing it all, the old timers were finally awake and missed nothing. The snapping noise had to come from their eyeballs popping open in unison along with broad smiles lighting up their faces. The next day we replaced the governor rope. The old guys on the couch were wide awake, slapping backs, poking each other in the ribs with all eyes glued to the elevator.

Russ kept up the good work by booking another jewel. This job had two running elevators and some history as well. Originally, Otis had installed two basement drum passengers and one geared freight. Years ago Otis had issued a notice that drum machines needed to be re-shackled every two years or so. An independent company was maintaining the equipment. The owner went to the maintenance company and they informed him it wasn't necessary to do the work. Otis knew what they were talking about and it wasn't long until the hoist ropes parted company and the car fell. To make matters worse, the governor failed as well. A woman was seriously injured and, justifiably, had her day in court. Time passed and the owner decided it was time to modernize one of the drum machines. A completely new elevator was installed using KM White equipment. A new basement traction machine was installed including overhead sheaves. During the installation the rigging for the temporary skip failed which resulted in serious injuries to both the Mechanic and his Helper. A few more years passed and the remaining drum machine became unserviceable. A small startup, independent company got the job due to their lowball price. They poor-boyed the installation by installing a two-speed AC machine in the overhead. They hung the grid resistors on the wall which later heated up and almost burned down the hotel. Their homebuilt controller used mag switches mounted in the hoist way for stepping, slowdowns and leveling. This five-stop car must have had 25 mag units mounted on the rail. To make this mess work, there had to be a fifteen-foot cam mounted on the car frame. This cam was so long it needed a hole in the machine room floor, which happened to be plywood. To make matters worse, the installer (I hate to bash a brother here) never saw a piece of pipe or a bender in his life. With all those mag switches there was flex everywhere, no straps, just tied together with strips of rags. Somehow this piece of junk was never written up for anything by the inspector. One reason could have been that he installed it. The guy even bragged about his first installation and how great it turned out. Over the years the hotel was turned into a retirement home. Both elevators shared the same lobby. Each had its own hall station. One of the first calls we got after taking over this job was that the residents were complaining about the service or lack of. Russ sent me over to see what I could do. Arriving at dinner time, it took about one minute to see the problem. First off, breakfast, lunch, mail call and dinner are the biggest events for the elderly residents. Two hall stations equaled four calls registered. Both cars stopped at every floor in both directions. To complicate matters, there was always an old guy who took over the elevator and provided preferential service to his friends. After explaining the problem to the Manager, he was a little miffed and told me Russ had told him the service would improve if he signed up with us. All I could say was, "Sorry" and went on to something I could fix or at least work on.

It wasn't long until the "callback from hell" came in for this account. The call came in that the old car was down and it was dinnertime. If I didn't get over and get it fixed pronto they were going to cancel the contract. So I had dinner, watched the Local and National news, got into my work clothes, gassed up my truck and headed to the call. Upon arriving I found a lobby full of old timers and a very irritated Manager. I picked the lock and saw that the car was down in the basement. I went to the basement and checked it out, pulled the doors closed and headed for the machine room. After all the fires from the grids and, not to mention, the under-engineered AC relays in the controller, the machine room looked like a burned out bunker straight out of a WWII movie. A good thing was that the raised concrete perimeter which surrounded the hoist way provided a comfortable place to sit in front of the controller. Another guy had provided a 2 inch cushion of rags already. Sitting down, I started checking this thing out. I had worked on this junk before and kind of knew my way around it. The selector indicated the car was at the bottom floor and ready to run. The DOL relay was out and should be in so I checked the coil and it was open. Not having one available, I pulled the relay in by hand and registered a top floor car call. The car started up, I let go of the relay and the car kept going. Good, I thought but something was missing. All that clatter of the selector relays was missing. The car kept running and I felt something brush the back of my shirt and "WHAM!" I immediately hit the disconnect and looked around. What hit the back of my shirt was the cam on the car as it came through the hole in the machine room floor. One more inch of butt-overhang would have been like a rectal exam by Bud with those short, thick fingers of his. The "WHAM" was caused by the crosshead hitting the overhead. The shackles were also sharing the machine room with me. "That's it, I'm outta here." I pulled the fuses and headed home. Well, it just gets better. After giving Russ the good news the next morning I headed on over to try to repair this dog. Too late, the route man had been there unaware of the previous night's disaster. Without calling the office he replaced the fuses, jumped the upper limit and sent the car down. Well, remember that long cam on the car? It was bent to hell and took out all 25 mag switches. All the switches and associated wiring ended up in the pit. I arrived five minutes later and it was more good news for Russ. It took a couple of days but we fixed it. We never did figure out why a burnt out DOL coil would drive this thing into the overhead. I replaced the relay and added an auxiliary (DOLA) so it would take both coils to fail for this to happen again. "Maybe" . . .

Russ did have his good moments and booked some good jobs. He sold fire service and earthquake modifications to an oil-fired power plant in El Centro. El Centro is over in the desert. There were two elevators in the plant, an EMCO and a Watson. Alex, our engineer in the Glendale office, did the circuit revisions for the EMCO and sent them over. The Watson only needed earthquake revisions. For this job I got a new Helper, Ernie. He was a good kid, good worker but a little green. We went over in the spring to start the job. The weather was great and the work went well. We got to know the guys working in the plant pretty well and noticed they were really working their tails off. We didn't know why until we returned in the summer to complete the punch list.

Summertime in EL Centro is Hell on Earth. The outside temperature is 110-120 degrees. The poor locals must seek refuge in the air-conditioned restaurants for their lunch breaks so they can consume gallons of ice tea. It's even too hot outside for the bugs; they like to hang out in the air-conditioned restaurants too. They crawl all over the ceilings and on occasion lose their grip and drop right into your drink like there's some kind of a diving competition. They must have practiced a lot because it seemed they never missed.

Returning to the plant we found why the guys were working their tails off last spring. The outside temperature was 110 and the inside was more like 125 degrees. Man, these guys went about their work like zombies. They shuffled from one task to another dragging a large fan. Before starting their work, they setup the fan so it would be pointing in the direction of where they'd be working. We were able to complete the punch list and get the hell out of town. The journey home was marred by our last evening's recreation.

Ernie and I had gone fishing in one of the canals the night before. The recommended bait was frozen mackerel. After an evening of drinking mass quantities of beer, cutting up bait, and wiping my hands on my shirt, little chunks of mackerel ended up all over the place, including inside my truck. The fishing was lousy so we headed back to the motel. Upon waking that morning with a sickly 7.0 hangover, we walked to the job (the motel was next to the plant) and completed our work. My truck that contained the little bits of previously frozen mackerel sat in the parking lot. The windows were closed tight and the inside was basking in the 110 degree heat. With the job done, it was time to start the hundred-mile journey to San Diego. I can't remember how far I had driven before I realized something was wrong, very wrong. My sickly 7.0 hangover immediately noticed the now-thawed mackerel. The contents of my stomach ended up all over my steering wheel and in the little nooks and crannies of the dashboard. All this, along with the previously frozen, now-thawed mackerel, would accompany me on the 100 mile journey through the 110 degree heat to my final destination . . . home.

While working in San Diego, I had the pleasure of working with two route men, Doug and Loy. Years before, Orv had pinned the name "Cowboys" on these two and it stuck until they both retired. Doug had come up through the ranks and was a Cracker Jack Serviceman. He was a busy guy and went through girlfriends and wives like we went through pager batteries and beer. He built houses, flew airplanes and spent his spare time waterskiing over at the Colorado River.

Loy was older. He'd been a Marine Engineer in the Navy during WWII. After the war he worked for Standard Oil all over South America. Loy was one the finest Mechanics I have ever known. To watch this guy with tools was something to behold. He spent his spare time riding dirt bikes over in the desert. A great sense of humor added to the pleasure of working with him. There was a drawback though ... his lower digestive system could, on command, emit the most disgusting gases and based on the intensity of the odor, I'm sure vapors as well. He used this talent not only for his own entertainment but for the entertainment of others as well. It came in very handy while doing everyday service duties at SDG&E ... "The GAS Company."

This customer was very touchy when it came to burnt-out indicator lamps and Loy did his very best to keep the customer satisfied. Here's the drill. As mentioned earlier, SDG&E had eight passenger cars that serviced twenty landings. The twenty landings included a basement. The basement was reserved for executive parking only, so the lowly Joe had no reason to make that journey. Loy had it worked out to a science. He would stand in the lobby and register a down-hall call; when an elevator answered the down call he would enter the car and register every car call. If there was a burnt-out lamp he would place the car on inspection, remove the car station cover, change the lamp, replace the cover and return the car to service. Normally, after registering all the car calls and ensuring all the lamps were okay, the car would travel down to the basement and cancel all the car calls that he had set. If he entered a car with no burnt-out lamps he would let it head to the basement. At this time he would unload all the noxious gases that had been stored in his lower colon for the last 12 hours. When the air inside of the elevator resembled the atmosphere of Venus, he allowed the car to continue to the basement. Loy figured if he held the car for a minute at the lobby there had to be at least one passenger, or if he was really on his game, there would be several waiting in the basement for that car to arrive. To check his work, he registered an up call in the lobby so he could observe the car's occupants when the doors opened again in the lobby. I've been there, I've seen it myself. Gotta tell ya, it is really something to see a car full of executives with strained looks, and eyes shifting from side to side not knowing just whom to blame.

Doug enjoyed every minute of Loy's antics and tried to imitate him but could never duplicate this Elevator Man Classic. Doug thought the world of Loy and was always at his side. Matter of fact, these two were inseparable.

It was a blast working with Loy, the king of the comeback. A typical example was when we responded to a less-than-satisfied Store Manager. Upon arrival we were confronted at the front door with tools in hand. "These escalators have been nothing but trouble and I called your Company about it," the Manager moaned. Loy looked him straight in the eye and said, "The only one who made out on that call was the phone company." A strange look came over the Manager's face and he stomped off shaking his head.

One morning we had half the steps piled up in front of the lower head when the Manager sauntered over and asked, "Just what the hell are you guys doing now?" Loy, with a straight face, replied, "It's obvious you don't know anything about escalators." "What do you mean? Of course I do. I've been managing department stores with escalators for twenty years." "Well sir, these escalators are equipped with the latest electricity-saving feature." "What's that?" the Manager asked. "Every morning we take all the steps out of the bottom here, take them back up to the top, put them back into the escalator so it can run all day." With a puzzled look the Manager muttered, "That's funny, we never had to do that in the other stores I've managed," and walked off. About twenty minutes later Loy's pager went off and he went to find a phone. He came back all smiles and said, "That was Amanda (our dispatcher) and she said she just received the weirdest call from the Manager over at Penny's." It wasn't that difficult to guess what his question was. She added, "You guys really do that!"

I learned a lot from Loy. There were some of his tactics that stuck with me the rest of my elevator career. His three approaches to troubleshooting were just plain and simple. To "Easter Egg It," was to look for parts lying in front of the controller. To "Humming Bird It," (note this only works with two identical cars or more sharing the same machine room) was to check the status of all the relays on a running car against the car that is broken down. And finally the most effective method of all was "T&E," "Trial and

Error," for all you laymen out there. Very simple and no laptop required.

John had booked a nice three-car job in La Jolla. I rounded up a great crew. Jimmy was my Helper, Jerry was my new TM and David was my 70% Helper. Haughton had engineered a package they called a GT 350. Basically it was their latest geared product with a Model V motor control. "The works in a drawer" was now history and it was replaced with PCBs that slid into a card rack in the controller. The job was moving along smoothly until our first speed bump. We had built the platforms, installed the cabs and the whole works were sitting on the car builders in the pit. The counterweight frames had just gotten to the jobsite. We setup a cathead at the top floor and rigged up the cwt frame with three-to-three rope blocks. Jerry and David were on the skip and were traveling along with the cwt frame as we hoisted it up. Jerry gave me a "stop!" signal and I stopped the cathead. He grabbed the rope block that was attached to the frame and shook it. The cwt frame then disappeared down the hoist way. All I could think about was the completed cab five floors below in the path of the runaway cwt frame. Jimmy reminded me some time later that during the frame's descent, I couldn't decide whether to head for the man lift or the stairs. He told me later that I ran from one to the other and finally hit the stairs to reach the same destination of the falling counterweight frame. Upon jumping on the car top I found absolutely nothing broken. Why this stroke of luck? We had filled the buffers with oil right after installing. The only damage was a pint of oil on the pit floor.

Doug called me one night and told me Russ suffered a serious heart attack and was in bad shape over at Scripps Hospital. The poor guy went through hell until he could go home. He retired with his two-bit Haughton pension and moved to the Oregon Coast. He was finally well enough to get in a little fishing and crabbing with his grandkids. Not a bad ending I guess, but unfortunately it got worse. We did keep in touch and one day he called me while almost crying to inform me his wife had left him after attending her high school reunion. His major complaint was that she might get part of his pension. She did, he died and that's the end of the story. It's rarely pretty.

With Russ gone and no heir-apparent in the near future, Dick, the Regional Manager, called and asked if I could take over the office.

We had one repair crew and about four routes plus a new Helper. We had nicknamed him "Gilligan" due to the striking resemblance to the guy in the TV show. He had a tendency to get a little excited and flustered just like the Gilligan on TV. His real name was Bob and he was turning out to be a damn good hand. One thing for sure, he was quick. Example … he had placed my toolbox on the crosshead on an elevator in a three-car group, on the twentieth floor that had a flattop. This car top was the flattest I have ever seen and the only saving grace was the escape hatch. We had renamed him Gilligan affectionately, but he never saw it that way and when he left the Company years later his parting shot was, "I'm going somewhere where I'm not Gilligan anymore."

Well, his new boss was a good friend and a phone call took care of that. His new company was a good company and even provided employees with coffee cups with their names on them. Upon arrival Bob was handed his brand new cup to break the ice but it didn't say "Bob." He never forgave me for that one. Back to the flatcar top . . . Bob, in a hurry, grabbed the toolbox by the handle and dumped all its contents on the cartop including all that miscellaneous small hardware that accumulates in its little nooks and crannies. Bob was like a madman gathering up everything thus, preventing a shower of hand tools and hardware from their twenty-floor journey down the hatch with a running car on each side. From that day on Bob never picked up anything by a handle used for carrying purposes. I'll wager to this day, when traveling he holds his suitcase with both hands and not the handle. Bob went on to do very well in the business and is well respected for his knowledge and work ethic. Now happily retired, you might even see Bob and his wife traveling the highways and byways in a motor home so huge it could have been used as a double in the Desi and Lucy movie, "The Long, Long Trailer."

I had been the LR in San Diego for a few months when the Company dispatched a junior salesman to help out with sales. Scott came right out of the Haughton Elevator finishing school and was a Toledo native to boot. He hit the ground running, looked around San Diego and after working in LA for awhile, figured San Diego was the place for him. Scott wrote his name on the old business cards Russ had left and was off and running. To this day Scott and I remain good friends. He now has an elevator consulting firm located in Orange County.

During our frequent visits to Toledo for schooling, I renewed a friendship with a route man, Tim, aka, "The Hawk." He had been a child star in his younger years and can still be seen as that little freckle-faced kid in those old Pat O'Brian tear-jerker's. He was a very funny guy with tons of stories about his time in the movie business. He told us a story about the Duncan Yo-Yo contest held on Hollywood Boulevard. While on the set for the movie "Kim," he was practicing his Yo-Yo skills when Errol Flynn appeared and asked if he could borrow his Yo-Yo. Tim gave Errol his Yo-Yo and after a few spins the string broke. Errol apologized and split. A week to the day of the broken Yo-Yo string incident, Tim received a large package in the mail. The package contained 1,000 Yo-Yo strings. The next time he saw Errol and expressed his gratitude, Errol said, "No sweat kid; I own a Yo-Yo string company in Australia." Tim grew up and his freckles were no longer needed in Hollywood. He had friends in the elevator business so he gave it a try. He made the right choice and went on to be a topnotch Serviceman.

After turning out as a Mechanic he had some of Haughton's show jobs in LA. He came up with fixes for Haughton controllers that had plagued other route men for years. Case in point, the Company used E26 coils for 208 VAC on most of the relays that stayed energized. The AC ripple would rattle the coils loose from the relay pole. After all this movement they would heat up and even burnout and start little fires in the controller. After awhile they would give out a certain type of odor you could smell even before you got to the machine room. Tim's fix was to wrap fiberglass tape around the pole and use a blue spring that had less tension than the factory-supplied green spring. This was only one example of the fixes he came up with to keep his jobs trouble-free. His customers loved him because his stuff ran like a top.

He had another story about a trouble call he answered on a job that had a deadbeat customer. The office instructed him to get cash in hand before fixing the elevator. Being young and anxious he let the customer talk him out of cash up front with the promise of payment upon the completion of the work. He fixed the elevator and presented the customer with a bill and the guy laughed in his face. Tim told the deadbeat he had to return to the machine room to pick up his tools. Upon leaving the machine room the customer approached him and asked him what he had in his hand. Tim replied, "This is the motor starter coil." The customer asked, "What does that do?" Tim replied, "This makes your elevator go up." "You mean my elevator won't run without it?" "Didn't say that," Tim said, adding, "It just won't go up." "Will it run both ways if I pay you now?" the customer asked. "You bet; I'll put it back in the minute you pay me." Customer: "Okay, what do I owe you?" "It will be three hours at our regular billing rate." "Wait a minute; you've only been here for thirty minutes." "The first two hours is our minimum and the extra hour is for me to reinstall the starter coil." The customer paid the three hours.

After a long and colorful career, Tim is now retired and enjoying life.

CHAPTER FIFTEEN
Off to Seattle

About this time my feet were starting to itch and the Pacific Northwest was calling. I dug in and waited for an opening. Scott was expanding his power base and the handwriting was on the wall. It wasn't long until the Company needed a Service Superintendent in Seattle and I was offered the job.

With bags packed and truck rented, it was off to The Great Northwest. Seattle was a typical Haughton operation. We had eight routes, two repair crews, a junior salesman, a secretary and a new Branch Manager, Harry. We had a nice office centrally located in Ballard that came with plenty of office space and a warehouse downstairs. I had been to Superintendent training en route to Seattle so I had enough information in my head to get started. We had a great crew, some with whom I had worked in Los Angeles. There was Bob who had trained under Dad and became a Cracker Jack troubleshooter and Adjuster. There was Jerry, a former Otis Adjuster. His knowledge didn't stop with just Otis. Bill and Dick, along with the other guys, more than held their own. Pat was one of the best repair guys I have ever known. Unfortunately, I lost Pat and Dick to other companies right off the bat. They had offers we just couldn't match. It was an early lesson, if a guy really wants to bolt, he will. If a guy needs constant stroking give it to him until you've had enough and when threatened with leaving, dial up your competitor and hand the guy the phone. You just have to adjust if a guy leaves you; it may be tough for awhile but sooner or later things will return to normal. I liked the job and the support Toledo provided. Harry, the new Branch Manager, was a good guy and we got along great. He was a hot salesman and would listen to his field personnel when it came to taking on new contracts. Although there were times he took on stuff that couldn't pay its own way.

There was one serious rub … wages. I was being pressured to give up my card but didn't and was holding out as long as I could. Union scale in Seattle was two bucks an hour better than what I was getting and the checkbook was starting to tell the tale. The Company painted all its Superintendents with the same brush. A guy in Cleveland was paid the same as a guy in LA or Seattle; big disparity in the cost of living. I waited until I was well enough entrenched and our bottom line was what Toledo wanted. Harry was in the same boat, his field people were making way more than he. Having an ally, we went to Spencer Street with our complaints. They ponied-up a token cost of living adjustment for management on the West Coast. Two things resulted; first, it was way short of covering the distance between the office guys and the field guys. Second, it pissed off all of our co-workers east of the Rockies.

Speaking of them, at least we found a way to the hearts of the guys working in Toledo. Coors Beer was not available in Toledo. The Coors pipeline consisted of our guys who went to Toledo for training. At that time Haughton was introducing several new product lines and it was necessary to train the guys so they could work on them. Every guy we sent to Toledo carried with him as check-in baggage one or two cases of Coors. After the first few cases of Coors crossed the Rockies the Seattle office was in all the thoughts and minds of the people in Toledo. We targeted the right people, parts, engineering and billing. The result was great; anything Seattle wanted or needed was immediately placed on the front burner.

Wages continued to be an issue so it was time to put a line in the water. In the meanwhile Harry and I were summoned to a sales meeting in Toledo. We both sat and listened to the new president tell all "they will increase their bottom line or else," all the while banging a wine bottle on the podium. The evening did have a highpoint when Harry and I were invited to come forth and receive an award for best cooperation between physical and administrative operations. Note here, the award was a result of the management field setup. Harry reported to his regional guy in LA and I reported to Toledo. I quit the next day. Harry quit a week later and joined me at US.

Western Elevator was started up in the late 50s by an Otis hand named Avery. Avery had worked with my father in years past and had brothers in the business. The story goes; he came up to Seattle from LA while working for Otis. In those days the majors had Seattle pretty well wrapped up. Avery went out on his own after making friends with people at Bon Marche. The Bon was a well-established department store throughout the Pacific Northwest. Their main store had enough equipment to support a one-man elevator company. Avery got started and took on the mix of elevators and escalators. The Bon had a hidden surprise for him that reared its head just when everything had settled down and Avery was making a buck or two.

The Otis gearless passenger cars had hollow shafts that were known to part company and one did just that. This repair would be on his dime and a big one at that. He borrowed money on his house to make the repair. What came out of this was a repair and coming up with a fix that involved a slug fitted into the shaft. It worked and he was on his way. Avery setup a warehouse with office space, hired the best men in the industry he could find and started manufacturing hydraulic elevators. He was in the right place at the right time. Seattle had a building boom going on and he was front and center to cash in. Western built and installed hundreds of hydros and many are still running today. They did it all, built car frames, controllers, pump units and some cabs. There was a complete parts department with a fulltime parts lady, Ann. He equipped a complete machine shop with the machinists to operate it. He had the best people and the infrastructure to support them and the rest was history. He installed a gas tank for the Company vehicles and, keeping up with employee relations, allowed his employees to gas up their own cars during the gas crisis.

During the late 70s US moved into the Pacific Northwest and started installing their equipment. There was work for everybody and the two companies existed side-by-side for a few years. US wanted to expand its base and it wasn't long until they made Avery an offer he couldn't refuse. It was US-Western for awhile and finally became US.

I had been talking with US for a few months; they tendered a final offer and it was time to jump ship. Their offer consisted of a car, guaranteed forty-hour week at 5% over scale. My job was to work as Service Superintendent in charge of repair and assisting Ken, the Service Manager. Ken had been hired by Avery back in the early Western years. He was one bright guy and ran a service department consisting of 25 routes. For me it was a big change from running eight routes, a repair crew or two, to running 25 routes, a shop man, two truck drivers and five repair crews. It was great and one of the best jobs I ever had. To begin with my repair crews were the best and gave eight for eight until the opening of hunting or fishing season. During these openings it became hard to find anybody to get the work done. I had a guy, Al, who was our escalator guy. There were a couple of young Mechanics who could work on the newer stuff. These kids Bryan and Jeff installed fire service upgrades and setup new jobs. Furthermore, I had access to Larry. He worked directly for Ken until I needed him. This guy was one of the brightest and best Mechanics I have ever worked with. He was somewhat of a Prima donna but well worth it when it came to push or shove. He was a guy who just went and did it after bitching and moaning in my office for fifteen minutes. A small price to pay for the work he turned out. These guys were the backbone of the whole operation. Having control of the repair crews, Adjusters and troubleshooters made the job fun to go to everyday. For the most part these guys weren't just employees but friends. I know this isn't supposed to work in the corporate world but it sure as hell did on Blakley Avenue. We had the whole State so my job included travel to Eastern Washington and the Olympic Peninsula. Drinking beer in a repair crew's truck on a Washington State ferry wasn't uncommon.

Along with our well-equipped shop was our shop man, "Karl." He was paid a little over Helpers' wages and had a card. He was an excellent welder and because he had a card we could send him to the field. Karl had one problem. He was lazy, I mean really lazy. He went home every night, exhausted. Why? He spent all day working his butt off at doing nothing. I was always on his tail about keeping the shop clean. He spent most of his day peeking through the little window in the door that led to the office so he could spot someone of authority coming down the hall headed for the shop. I know there were days he went home with a whiplash after bending his neck all day to stay out of sight. He was a longtime employee and in spite of his attempts to screw the dog all day, he came in handy when we needed a welder or fabricator.

We had several truck drivers over the time I spent at US. Most were young guys looking to get into the field. Some did some did not. These guys were responsible for securing their loads before driving out to the job sites. Again, most did but one didn't. The one who didn't was Craig, nicknamed "Craigmo." I would get complaints about shortages from the Mechanics on the jobs. It seemed Craigmo had more than his share of beefs. We found out this guy couldn't tie a square not if his life depended on it. The chickens came home to roost when I was in a construction delay on US Hwy 2 headed for Eastern Washington to check on a job. While sitting in my car going nowhere, I saw a piece of rusty green US gutter lying alongside the road. It was stop and go for the next hour or two. During that time I saw several more pieces of gutter and even a car stile. Most of the stuff I saw on my trip belonged to the job I was going to visit. This guy had scattered rusty green sheet metal all over the State of Washington. We had to let Craigmo go.

Craigmo's replacement was an older guy who was a friend of Karl's ... we should have known. But we were busy and needed a body, pronto. Well, it wasn't that long until Olie became "Dufus." This guy had pretty simple stuff to do and normally did okay. We started buying 55-gallon drums of a product called Luberzoil. This stuff was an industrial hydraulic oil conditioner. It worked like magic when added to a hydro tank. The mix was one gallon to 50 gallons of hydro oil. The problem was getting it out of the drum into gallon jugs because it had the consistency of STP and was as slippery as Rottweiler drool. The shop was cold during the winter so the filling of the gallon jugs could be a long process. Well, Dufus tipped the drum over on its stand, placed a gallon jug under the tap and opened it. All is well, right? Go find something else to do while the gallon jug fills up. The gallon jug should fill up in around five minutes at the current temperature. He found something else to do all right; it was 4:30 p.m. so he went home. By 7:00 a.m. the next morning our shop could have qualified as an EPA superfund site. It took all hands all day to clean up the shop floor and Dufus wasn't one of them.

The backbone of the modernization and repair business at US was Harry. He served in the Navy during WWII. Prior to entering the elevator business he worked as a journeyman carpenter for the Bureau of Land Management (BLM). He had started with Western and was still going strong when US hit the scene. During his early days with Western his service route consisted of a bunch of old water hydros in South Seattle. All he needed to keep his route running was a few leathers for three-way valves. Traveling light, he bought a motor scooter to service his route. He turned in his mileage just like the other guys and this drove Ken nuts. Ken could never get over the fact that Harry was getting into his pocket with his little scooter. Harry ended up waving the Standard Agreement book in Ken's face and that was that. Harry and I worked great together. The best part was when he would rush into my office and exclaim, "This is a Slab-Sided Holdover." Note here, "A Slab-Sided Holdover" is a large salmon that missed a run and was the biggest fish in his school. A Slab-Sided Holdover was always a great sales lead. To get to the perspective job we would either jump in the car or even jump on a plane to get out and get that signed contract. At US we didn't have the corporate restraints and were pretty much on our own. An example of a Slab-Sided Holdover was the Bon store in Yakama which had an old Peele escalator which had piled up. Haughton had already been there and had shipped the material necessary to complete the job. To keep Haughton honest, the Bon called us for a quote and Harry and I grabbed a plane and showed up that afternoon. We checked out the broken escalator and had a price for them in two hours. Our price was half of what Haughton wanted, we got the job and had it manned in two days ... made money too!

The Bon store in Yakama called again and asked if we could come over and look at the escalator because there had been a serious accident. A child had lost a toe. The shoe department was right next to the bottom of the down escalator. This old Peelle had rubber half-inch step treads with chunks missing. The child, while barefoot, had run over to the escalator and wrapped his toes over the comb plate and lost a toe. Note: the Bon was maintaining their own equipment at the time. Haughton had given them a price to replace the bad step treads with original equipment. The end result was that the half-inch step treads were still there.

Working for US and not Haughton gave us the freedom to pursue another course of action. The step treads were sheet metal pans with cast-rubber treads. We removed the steps, the step tread pans and cast new, narrower, rubber step treads using a standard comb plate as a guide. We had a company in Seattle that had already done this type of work for us. It worked and we made money again!

The guy who did most of our escalator work was Al. He was one of the best hands we had, A Good Ole Boy, to say the least. He was as steady as they can get and my fishing buddy to boot. He didn't have much in the way of tools but he still managed to get the job done with a couple of rounded off screwdrivers and a pair of old, rusty channel locks. He is now happily retired and catching fish all over Washington State.

Emergencies happened all the time. A week never went by without Harry standing in the doorway of my office, waving a sheet of paper with a huge smile all over his face. Working with Harry was a highpoint in my elevator career.

A bag manufacturing plant in South Seattle had an old two-stop drum that was on the safeties with the hoist rope shackles pulled out of the car hitch plate. The other problem was that the cast iron gear was cracked. Haughton had been there and quoted them on a new gear and all the necessary work to get the elevator in service again. The plant called us and we were there in thirty minutes. The gear is still there and the ropes and counterweights are gone. They liked our quote and we starting drilling a hole for a jack in two days. I had just the guy for the job . . . "Jess."

Jess was a 6'6" Dane weighing in at 100 pounds dripping wet. His lack of bulk never deterred him from getting the job done. With arms and legs as thin as toothpicks and twice the length of an average guy, he was able to use his limbs as giant levers. This guy had more leverage than a kid's teeter-totter.

He was a little on the temperamental side and required more than his share of stroking. It was always, "I'm going to quit; I'm going somewhere where they give me wan and tool." An English translation would be . . . I'm going somewhere where they are going to give me a van and tools. On the bright side, he was one of the best Mechanics I have ever had the pleasure of working with. A former machinist, he could weld water with a damp welding rod. We used him on our jack jobs but he really excelled on motor and bearing work.

Sorry to say I did lose Jess to a new yellow Dodge van full of brand new tools.

Frank aka, "Spanky" was probably the oldest elevator man still working in the business. This guy didn't have a light duty job like a service route. He did heavy repair at the age of seventy. I mean heavy repair. He had been a master rigger at the shipyards during WWII. As a young man he even worked on a whaling ship. He had worked for Otis for many years and on every major installation and modernization they did in the Pacific Northwest. He had been around for so long, he had modernized jobs that he had originally installed; not just a few times either. He worked the Bon store downtown three times, starting with the original car switch installation, adding signal panels and finally the complete changeover to automatics.

He could do up to four re-shackles a day. Some of the elevators he re-shackled might not be running when he left but he still got the rope work done. When visiting him, he would always throw the cork in the fireplace which meant we were bound to finish that bottle. When he did jobs at a senior citizen building, the women were all after him. I visited him on one of these jobs and found him in a chair in the community area surrounded by old ladies. He had his driver's license out and was showing it to all the women because they didn't believe he was in his seventies. He did finally retire on my watch and it was the end of an era.

Life was good. Wages went to 12% plus a bonus. Harry (Harry from Haughton) asked me if I would take over construction. I did and he provided an assistant, Bob. Bob was a young guy who had grown up in Eastern Washington. He was very good at his job and entertaining as well. A funny guy, he could turn a dull story into a very humorous tale. Friday afternoon was best because I would get him a tall can of Fosters lager from the 7-11. Halfway through the lager he became a comedian who was fit for a standup comic act.

It was a great job and there was always some problem to solve because the junk US shipped out their back door was horrible. We had machine problems and had to deal with Link Belt, a gearbox turned into an elevator machine borrowed from a conveyor belt. The dynasty was Link Belt, then came son of Link Belt, Kone Drive, and another misplaced gearbox that should be running a crane, Kalicko, another jewel that ended up with a bent worm gear after the first full load safety test. The new mufflers were welded up pipe that resembled a radiator used to heat old buildings. These things worked great for awhile and would just stop muffling. This bunch of pipe welded together would work until the air was purged from the system. We tore them all out and replaced them with mufflers purchased from Freeman. It wasn't long until the factory was doing the same thing.

We lived with problems like this and got paid to get it as right as could be. Twenty jacks in the ground provided a lot of work for my crews. The problem here is that we had short jacks, long jacks and jacks in the wrong place.

The hits just kept on coming. We had installed a four-stop duplex over in Bellevue. These were fast, high-capacity hydros, with big jacks with huge tanks. The building was a first-class place. The beautiful lobby had a giant Turkish carpet set in a perimeter surrounded by terrazzo. The machine room was at the same level. The first disaster, the machine room got so hot the fire sprinkler went off. Normally not a big deal but in this case it was a really big deal. First problem, the sprinkler was directly over the tank. That wouldn't have normally caused concern. Second problem, the last genius on the job left the tank lid off. The tank flooded and 75 gallons of a water-oil mixture flowed out of the tank. Well, it had to go somewhere. It did, it flooded the first floor. The good thing was that there wasn't the whole 75 gallons to clean. The drywall took care of that. Every space that was dry walled on the first floor had a brown stain half way up from the floor. The expensive carpet looked like a skating rink.

We are on the hook to replace all the drywall and save the Turkish carpet. We had had some major oil spills in the past and I used a carpet company named, believe it or not, "The Fuzzy Wuzzy Rug Company." They were on the ball and had removed and cleaned the carpet in a few days. The work is progressing with the carpet replaced and the sheet rockers doing their part.

US, in their infinite wisdom, had come up with a little gadget that was supposed to act as a recovery system. Problem was the outlet line in the machine was installed below the oil level. It was piped into the manifold by the factory. It recovered all right and siphoned the oil out of the tanks into the already-flooded pits, out onto the lobby where our (by now we owned it) newly cleaned carpet resided. Call "Fuzzy Wuzzy" again. They removed, cleaned and reinstalled the carpet. They had a tough time due to the fact that the carpet was starting to shrink.

We did it! Everything was getting back to normal. The recovery system was trashed and all we needed to do was get the oil out of the pits. I sent a crew over with a pump, empty drums and a truck full of Drysit. They got started and were well into the job and then the hose blew off the pump. These guys are busy in the pit and by the time they knew something was amiss, twenty gallons of oil was sprayed all over our carpet. "Call Fuzzy Wuzzy" for the third time. They cleaned it, but it was several inches smaller than it used to be. This time the rug didn't make it. Oh well …

We were self-insured at the time and were going to be out big bucks when a miracle happened. I sent one of the young Adjusters to tune up the elevators and he happened to look at the sprinkler heads. "The sprinkler contractor had installed the wrong fuses." Way too low of a temperature for an elevator machine room. These fuses belonged out on the patio. At least US didn't have to cough it all up for the new drywall and our beloved carpet.

Our boss was Lloyd, the Company's enforcer and ax-man. Prior to my arrival on the scene, Ed was the Branch Manager. He picked Lloyd up at the airport one morning, bought him breakfast and drove him to the office. Upon entering the office Lloyd said to him "Give me your keys, you're through." Lloyd was the terror of all Managers and Superintendents.

While in San Diego on business I happened to walk by his office and he motioned for me to come in. He was on the phone yelling at some manager about his bottom line. While the poor guy on the other end was trying to save his job, Lloyd muffled the phone with his hand and said, "Hi, Jim. It's great to see you and how's the family?" He put his hand up and went back to reaming out that poor chump on the phone. This continued a couple of more times until the end of the phone conversation. Lloyd went back to the niceties and gave me the keys to his car, so I had transportation while I was in town.

Seattle, along with the whole State of Washington, decided it was time to install fire service Phase One and Two on most of the elevators in the State. For us this would turn into a "Cash Cow." Using my experience from San Diego we started to engineer a standard fire service overlay panel. Using the basic circuitry Haughton used, we installed the first hardwired version on two Haughton cars in Pullman, Washington. From there we cranked out some more hardwired version that was installed by my guys, Jeff, Dick and Brian. After they installed the hardwired version we all got together and came up with a new version of an overlay that would work on most equipment. From there it was off to San Diego again with our drawings, so they could design a printed circuit board that contained all the relay sockets, jumpers and terminals for optional dry contacts.

It took a couple of tries to get the right size foil. The end result was a fire service overlay in a can that mounted on the side of the controller which would work on most elevators.

Harry, our salesman, was retiring. Running construction and repair was starting to wear me down. I had been talking to Skip over at Haughton about a job. He informed me they had plenty of mod work coming up and the job was mine if I wanted it.

I received word through the grapevine that Bud was seriously ill and the outlook was grim. I was in Seattle and he was in LA. I called Harry (Harry of Haughton) who was now the Regional Manager in LA and asked if he needed a job checked out. He said, "Hell, yes and you can pick up your plane tickets at the airport." Upon arriving in LA, I checked in with Harry, got my marching orders, and it was off to Sunset Boulevard to survey an upcoming modernization. San Diego also knew I was in LA and they had me survey another job on the West Side. On my own for a couple of hours it was off to see Bud. I met him at his home in Norwalk and spent most of the day there. It had been years since I had last seen him and it saddened me to see him in this condition. We talked of family, friends and old times. I returned to Seattle the following day. To this day I sincerely thank Harry and US Elevator for an afternoon with a friend, mentor and "One Hell of an Elevator Man." Bud passed away a few weeks later.

I left US and returned to "Mother Haughton." Haughton was now Schindler-Haughton and my new work shirts said, "Jim, Twenty Years of Service." I was kind of proud of that fact. First job up was Seattle City Hall; it was originally installed by Haughton in the 60s using regulator generator motor control along with B3 Vernier selectors. Working this job put me right in my comfort zone because I used to install this stuff back in the old days. My Helper was Chuck. This guy was an ace and a real asset to me due to the fact I just picked up the tools again. We replaced the old equipment with Accu-Flight motor control and a 1092 MC group supervisory system. About this time the Company put Chuck out as a Mechanic, which was well-deserved. I got a new Helper, Kim. A good guy but he had a tough time with me because I was so used to having Chuck. I heard later that Kim turned out to be a good elevator man. The job finished up and turned out to be a sweet install.

There was a problem . . . my big boss, Ken. He was an old-time Haughton employee who ran the Spokane office. He had become a District Manager and thus, I had to answer to him. He was one of the old hard-line manager types who had never worked in the field and thought the field guys were out to screw the Company. He even laid all his field employees off during the holiday season. His reasoning behind this was, "Well, you guys aren't going to work anyway because of the holidays." He got away with it because there weren't that many jobs available in Spokane.

We went back to City Hall to shorten the hoist ropes. We started the first car and discovered a serious problem. Most elevator men who have been around for awhile have run into this situation, especially on two-to-one installations. The ropes look okay but when a three foot length is bent back onto itself, the rope shatters. Well, we tested a length that was cut off for the shortening and it basically pulverized. Time for new ropes, I ordered them up and we went ahead and installed them. When Ken saw the bill, he went into orbit. Ken hit the ceiling and was in the process of ripping me a new one. I presented a length of the old rope and performed the bend back test right in his face. Ken was never a problem again.

Next was helping out at Smith Tower. This job had forty stops and was installed in 1914. For years it was the tallest building West of the Mississippi. This was some job, Otis gearless machines with 4F controllers. The elevators were originally powered by the 200 volt streetcar lines. After the city tore up the tracks, huge banks of rectifiers were installed in the basement. It was kind of eerie being in the machine room with running cars and only the sound of the controllers. Wayne was running the job and knew his stuff. Our job was to remove the existing birdcage cabs, have them re-plated, replace the Otis 4F controllers with O Thompson controllers and install Knickerbocker microprocessor controls.

A panel in the cab, similar to a car station, would tell the operator where to go just like the old enunciators. The last part is where I came in. We started up the new microprocessor system and it was a disaster. We never did get them to work no matter what we tried. We grounded, shielded and separated microprocessor circuits from the 220 volts DC that was all over the place. The poor guy from Knickerbocker finally flew back East with his microprocessors checked as baggage.

Our next project was the Center Building in Downtown Seattle which started out as two buildings with a hole in the wall that connected the machine rooms. There were four 80U passenger cars along with a car switch service car. The history of this building was all over the machine room. All the paperwork that covered past work was still there. The passenger cars were originally car switch control. Years ago Otis came in, retained the original starter panels and added 140M selectors and auxiliary panels for each car. They installed the group supervisory and overtime wait panels in the corner of the second machine room. The machine room was cramped as hell to begin with and here we are adding eight more panels for the microprocessor overlay.

Gene was my Helper on this job and was a great hand. This guy's wiring was some of the prettiest work I have ever seen.

We had to cut each car out for the overlay. After you have done a few of these jobs, you learn to keep your ears open. When it gets quiet there is a problem (this usually means one or several of the cars have quit running) especially right before noon. This happened to us more than once and when it did we had to backtrack as fast as hell. Gene had misunderstood me and cut the wires at an auxiliary panel for the wrong car … one that was still in service, poor guy was sick about it.

The system ran all right but on occasion would crash and run on the so called "Flub Circuit." The way this circuit worked was, if the computer crashed, all cars would chase any hall call and when the call was answered, they stopped at the nearest landing. This happened quite often until we hooked up the system ground to the building's plumbing down on the next floor and like magic, no more crashes. We got lucky on this one.

Clair operated the service car in the building. On occasion she would park her steed up on the tenth floor with the doors closed and listen to our conversations during lunch. Gene picked up on her eaves dropping and wanted to pull a prank. We started talking about her by saying she was a nice-looking older woman. A day later, upon entering her elevator, we noticed some very significant changes. Her hair was done, nice makeup and nice duds. She looked great and Gene and I were very proud of ourselves.

The Company had booked another overlay. It was a four-car group installed by Montgomery and modernized by Westinghouse in the 60s. We were to install a 1092 microprocessor overlay. All of the original machine room equipment stays. All we were doing was plugging into it here and there to tell the old system what to do. This was another cramped install. The best way to handle this is to get the inspector out and ask him where he wants the new equipment installed. We were in good shape because the State inspector was a good guy and spent years in the field. I was lucky enough to get Chuck back for this job and seeing how he lived right down the street, he was happy to be there.

Things happen on jobs that may come up again years down the road. This is one of those things. Our work here included five-year safety and buffer tests. We checked the pit prior to the tests and found one counterweight buffer compressed. It could have been compressed for months, years or during our time on the job. These were Montgomery buffers rated at about 500 feet per minute. During the tests the cars hit hard, basically the buffers didn't work that well. One car hit so hard that the newly installed Innovation Industries door protective device sheared right off the car door and ended up dangling by its cord. We got through the tests by the skin of our teeth and I assume the equipment is still in use. I ran into these particular buffers on my next job.

CHAPTER SIXTEEN
Sacramento

The Company had booked a big job in Sacramento. This job would be the largest project I had worked outside of new construction. The Water Resources building (WR) was in Downtown Sacramento. There were a total of ten elevators that serviced fifteen stops. The layout was one sixteen-stop service car, five fifteen-stop 700 FPM high-rise cars and four 500 FPM low-rise cars.

The work involved would be a complete tear-out and replacement of all machine room equipment including the machines and the safeties for the high-rise cars. The new machines would require new hitch plates both car and counterweight. The work on the low-rise was the same as the high-rise with the exception of replacing the machines. All new fixtures, hoist way door equipment and door operators would be provided on all nine cars.

The way this job had come about was that Haughton had furnished all the new equipment except for the operators, which were MAC, to a local independent company that had won the contract for the modernization work. These guys were booking work all over Central California and Nevada. The problem was, they were getting paid without doing the work. The inevitable happened, they went belly up. So now the bondholder that provided the bond for WR was left holding the bag. The new equipment was warehoused across the river in West Sacramento. The bondholder came to Haughton and asked if they would finish the work. At this point, my flag was flying pretty high with the Company and WR became my job.

There were three guys on the job when I arrived with my tools. Dave was a very experienced Mechanic and a great wrench as well. He did have two problems; he was melodramatic as hell and he couldn't keep his mouth shut. The worst thing an occupant of the building could ask is, "How's it going?" The following conversation could go on forever or at least until lunch or quitting time. The occupants started using a move we called, "The Dave One Step." The way it worked was, during a conversation, each time Dave was distracted or turned his head, the unfortunate building occupant would take one step away. In awhile Dave was shouting due to the distance, making conversation impossible. The building occupant could then make his escape. He would spend fifteen minutes explaining to me why he installed a green jib rather than the standard white jib supplied for the job. He just couldn't keep his mouth shut.

The exhaust fan in the machine room needed to be reversed. The chief engineer had informed us that he had replaced the fan motor. Dave went off on him, "You didn't have to replace the motor; all you had to do was reverse two wires." This was right in front of all the guy's men. I could have killed him. It was useless, he just didn't get it.

All in all, Dave was a great guy with a good heart and was a pretty damn good elevator man. He left us to start another job across town. At quitting time with a lobby full of people he shows up with his hardhat and safety belt. One of the building occupants happened to ask, "What's all that stuff?" "Just working that high iron," he replied. This was a "Snicker" that came up again and again. Dave has now retired and is living the good life last I heard.

Dave's Helper was a younger guy named Terry. This kid had been around and was a great hand. Easy to get along with and he did the best impressions of Dave which entertained us during our workday. He was a Down Easterner and had the accent to go with it. Someone else liked him too. A girl started stalking him during our lunch and coffee breaks. She would intercept him at every corner. As the job progressed so did their relationship and they became "The Talk of WR."

Tracy was a younger guy who had bounced around the business for quite awhile. His dad was like "Mr. Otis" and he still couldn't hang on to a job. I took Tracy under my wing and started training that went back to the old school. Don't be afraid to chew ass for screw-ups and heap praise for good work. This worked for him and I found out if you laid out the work for him, he could do it as well as any Mechanic. His work was done right and his wiring was neat, or you could say "down-right pretty." He never made a wiring mistake during the entire job. I gave Tracy the waste management job which he tackled with enthusiasm. Waste management meant complete housekeeping performed every Friday. He kept our job clean as can be and continued to perform this chore on his own without any further instruction. I feel Tracy learned a lot while working with me and he proved it by becoming a first-rate Mechanic.

The extra Helper was Brett. Here was a guy who marched to a different drummer. I setup the dope sheets and he did the majority of the wiring. He did a good job with few mistakes. He did have one serious problem. He had some kind of rabbit business that required working most of the night on one night a week. After working on that one night a week, he would show up late or not at all on the following morning. This was becoming a problem so I had to have the Company let him go. They did and the next day I was confronted by his complete family in the high-rise machine room. They all had hang-dog looks and there was nothing else I could do but take him back. From that day on he was never late and showed up every day.

With Dave gone we could set Terry up as a TM. Needing another Helper, we picked this Korean guy named N-jay. This guy's command of the English language left a lot to be desired. Fortunately for us, Terry could understand him. He was a good Helper and a nice guy with a crappy home life. His wife disliked him so much that when he came home at night she would turn out the front porch light as he pulled into the driveway. His broken English provided much entertainment for all. I asked him who he had worked for prior to WR. His answer was "Mongo Mary." As a new arrival to Local 8 (San Francisco) and hearing that all types were members I assumed that "Mongo Mary" was just another gender-confused member of the local. Terry stepped in and said, "He means Montgomery." Another time was on a Monday morning when I asked him what he did over the weekend, he replied, "I went to yo-so-mea-tee." Translation was Yosemite. We all really liked N-jay and he profusely thanked us for not referring to him as, "You stupid chink." Time passed and Terry and N-jay were a perfect team.

The local guys were somewhat leery about an outsider running a large job on their turf. They watched us like a hawk. Every day at quitting time a Dover van was parked within eyesight of the building's entrance with the occupant counting heads. I don't know what he was looking for, but it was time to have some fun. I instructed some of the guys to use the side exit on alternate days to screw up this guy's headcount. The stalker saw the humor in my tactics and we became friends.

The problem the local guys had at this time was "Roy." He owned a small company that had just been purchased by Schindler-Haughton. He was probably the most unscrupulous individual in the elevator business. He was a former teacher turned elevator man with a long history of near-criminal acts. I had heard about this guy when I was working for US in Seattle. He was working for US in the Bay Area and building owners were calling the US office to get their elevator fixed. When the Serviceman's time hit the office there was no account to charge it to. Roy had been stealing new elevators, part by part and installing them on his own time. He was able to get away with it because the missing equipment was treated as a shortage and just reordered. They investigated him and found out he had been doing the same thing when he worked for the phone company. The phone company and US came very close to filing criminal charges. The Union was all over him, but to Roy it was like water running off a duck's back. He was also stealing our new equipment from our warehouse until I caught him in the act but all we could do was bar him from entry. The Union had their hands full, and I couldn't blame them for watching me because Roy and I were basically working for the same Company.

The job's progress started to slow down. In fact, we were "Dying on this Hill."

To make matters worse, my Superintendent was Joe. This guy, in my opinion, was the most worthless individual who was ever in the elevator business. The Company was hiring retired military guys as Superintendents and they picked this guy up. To begin with, he was full of crap. You knew he was lying when he had his mouth open. According to him he had won the Vietnam War single-handedly and was the best thing that had ever happened to Schindler-Haughton Elevator Company.

We spent hours and hours recalibrating governors that should have been fixed in the factory. To make matters worse, the Company had re-engineered Accu-Flite and turned it into a monster. The building had a zillion-kilowatt radar antenna that would wreak havoc on our motor control electronics. There were small power supplies embedded in the system that, when exposed to radar radiation, would screw up and shut the car down. I went to Joe with all of this and more and his reply was, "I need you to get a number of the hall paint so we can touch up the wall after installing the new fixtures." "For Christ's sake Joe, do it yourself, it's your job." It came time for safety and buffer tests on the low-rise cars. I had been around these buffers before and knew they didn't work. According to him and the consultant, I didn't know what I was talking about. "Okay, you got it," and we ran a preliminary full-load, full-speed test. The car hit so hard and the ropes came so far out of their retainers that one of them snagged on the counter weight frame and broke. Joe and the consultant knew about this and their answer was, "Change the seals in the buffer." There aren't any seals in these buffers." We had just rebuilt these elevators and fearing further equipment damage, and not to mention passenger safety, I did the only thing I could; I called in Chuck, the State inspector on the next test.

Chuck got into the adjacent pit, and I ran the test. The car hit so hard that Chuck condemned the buffers on the spot. We had eight new Haughton buffers on the loading dock in two weeks. Joe was still pissed due to the fact that the Company had negotiated a low labor rate on change orders, never mind the equipment and the safety of the elevator-riding public.

The job drug on and I was losing my grip and there were serious changes going on in my personnel life. I was burnt out, drinking too much, and one day I lost my job. Everything happens for a reason but a good thing can come out of every bad thing. One of the best things that ever happened to me was that layoff.

I still had a pretty good rep and US picked me up to do a couple of small mods. They went badly and that was the end of that job. A small independent called me and I worked a few small jobs and they ran out of work and I was back on the bench.

Reliable picked me up for a mod job at the Department of Education. It was an Otis three-car group and we were going to replace the door equipment, motor control and fixtures along with doing some cab work. It wasn't ready to start yet so I went to LA to work in the service department. It was a great job for the most part; all I did was answer trouble calls. I worked mainly on the West Side and this was my old stomping ground as a teenager. It was cool to be back in familiar surroundings.

The job in Sacramento started with me, Dave, Bobby and Tim. I have to admit I learned a thing or two from Dave and Bobby. The motor control and group supervisory system was supplied by Swift. This was great stuff, easy to install and setup. Our supervisor was Jess, a New Yorker, who had owned his own company back there. He knew his stuff and I learned a lot from him. This job was a fun one and Tim was a great Helper.

To break up the monotony we would briefly stop work and try the "Old Dollar Bill Trick." We would slide a dollar bill out onto the lobby floor from under the hoist way door and wait for a pigeon. The pigeon reaches for it and as soon as we saw their hand, the bill was quickly pulled back into the hoist way. One buck did produce some results, but we found we had much better luck with a fiver. One of our victims had it figured out and would approach the entrance from the side, step on the bill so when we pulled it back in all we got was about twenty cents worth. We never pulled this trick on his floor again.

A few months into the work, here comes Jess with a handful of paper, moaning and groaning about our progress. He attempted to crack the whip but to no avail. You have to do the job right. I asked him if we would be on time if the Company had bid the job the same as the next lowest bidder. His answer was "yes" and there were no more complaints about our progress. A note here, when you're bidding against the majors and you come in way under them, there has to be a reason. "You're too damn low." The job had finished and I found myself back on the bench again until the "Elevator Gods" really smiled upon me this time.

CHAPTER SEVENTEEN
Monterey

While working at Water Resources, I met a local Mechanic, Jimmy. This Guy would turn out to be one of my best friends. He was a super Mechanic, smart as a whip and a funny guy. We spent our afternoons after work at Gilhouli's Bar or on my patio drinking beer and building elevators. I think what he admired the most about me, was my full size trash can in the center of the living room. Don't get me wrong, I kept a clean pad and the can had a fresh plastic bag at all times. He was also impressed with the baseball bat next to the front door used to discourage unwanted visitors. I spent my weekends working on projects at his house … pouring concrete for his swimming pool, etc.

I had been on my butt for a few months with no prospects. Things were slow until Jimmy called me one night and informed me that an independent company was looking for a man to work in Monterey, CA. "Who was it?" I asked and he said it was a guy named Harold who owned Tri County Elevator Company. After catching my breath, I told him that I had known Harold when he was a Serviceman working in Las Vegas. Jimmy gave me a contact number which I called immediately. Harold and I talked and he remembered me from those days and asked me to send him a resume. It seemed like years while I waited for his call. The call came in and I got the job. I always wanted to live and work in Monterey and here was my chance.

As it turned out, I was replacing a man who had been killed on the job, "Mike." Mike answered an overtime call, a two-stop Tri County Elevator. The problem was that it had a bad leveling inductor. The leveling and slowdown inductor were mounted to a can that had a light fixture mounted on the hinged cover. He opened the cover and was reaching around the can to replace the inductor. The hinged door that had open 120VAC terminals for the light swung closed and the 120VAC terminal touched his wire framed glasses. His left arm was wrapped around the can and completely grounded. He died shortly thereafter. As the hours passed his wife became concerned and called the answering service to see if they knew his last location. They informed her that his last call was over on Cass Street. The other route man, Don, was called and he went to the building. Upon arrival Don looked through the door gap and saw that the car top light was on and saw Mike's green shirt. Before doing anything he called 911 and then picked the lock and opened the door. He checked Mike and there was nothing he could do. The Paramedics arrived and pronounced Mike dead at the scene. Mike left a large family.

The lawsuits followed and it was determined that it was just an accident. Harold did start shielding the exposed circuitry on new installations. He also paid Mike's wife a year's worth of wages, which added to the Workers Comp settlement.

My first day was spent getting familiar with my new route. I was given a brand new Company van. It was time for my first day and, not to mention, a test.

The Marriot was my anchor job in Monterey. It had five 10-stop Dover composites and one hydro. They had been trying to fix one of the service cars that had been down for a week. It was all mine, my new job was on the line. I got lucky and had the car running again in two hours. I had a new job . . .

Tri County was started by Harold in Santa Barbara and the Company grew to Ventura and Monterey Counties. They did most of their manufacturing with the exception of door equipment, jacks and cabs. He had borrowed some ideas from the Haughton West Coast Hydros. He did get rid of the stepping switch and used a relay inductor selector. He had been installing his elevators for years, and they were all over the place. They were great little units and reasonably trouble-free. My route consisted of most of the hotels and the local hospital. We had a definite advantage over the other guys because we had two fulltime guys in the area.

I soon became LR and had most of the responsibility for setting up repair crews and working with the salesman, "Earl." He had owned a meat company in Chicago. He sold it and migrated to the West Coast. He was a hot high-pressure salesman. There was a saying going around about him. "Would you buy a used car from this man?" He did get the work.

Over the years, I was able to work with many different guys and ended up the "last man standing."

Don was the other Mechanic when I arrived. He was a good, dependable wrench and we had a good workplace relationship. His route was the out route which included Salinas, Watsonville and Santa Cruz. It turns out, he had quite a past.

Years ago, while working in San Diego for Westinghouse, the Business Manager paid us a visit. The reason for his trip was to say, "If the police asked any questions about a fellow member, keep your mouth shut." Some twenty-odd years later I found out what he was talking about. One day while having lunch with Don I heard the whole story.

Don was working in LA and frequented a bar where he and the barmaid were way more than friends. At that time he was out of control; drinking, doing drugs and being just an all around tough guy. This story was unraveling because he had been born-again.

One afternoon he went to the bar where his girlfriend worked and found some guy hitting on her. Less than pleased, he informed the suitor that he was messing around with private property. The other guy wasn't giving up easily and became physical. After a few blows Don broke a beer bottle and stabbed the guy in the throat. The injured man staggered all over the bar room spewing blood from his wound until he hit the floor. The place had been empty during all this, so the only witness was the barmaid. She swore to secrecy and Don left the scene for the last time. He went on to tell me that after being born-again he went to the LA District Attorney and confessed his crime. The DA told him that with the case being so old and no one around to press charges to forget it and go home. It's funny how things can just run their course. He was having back problems which required surgery. After his surgery he retired and bought a home in Idaho.

Tyrone was another guy who worked with me, a great wrench but his mind was on another planet. It was like he had his own little company on the side. Well, guess what …that's exactly what he did have. Harold had to let him go.

Fred was Harold's troubleshooter, a smart knowledgeable hand but handicapped by his size. He also suffered narcolepsy and it wasn't surprising to find him asleep in the machine room. He didn't do it on purpose; he just couldn't help it. I would get calls from customers about the big guy in a Tri County shirt asleep in their lobby. One time he fell asleep on the lawn in front of the Salinas Courthouse and a good Samaritan called the aid car. He was kind of high-maintenance because he couldn't drive so I had to haul him around. It was worth it because once I got him setup on a job he usually fixed it. He's now retired and participates regularly in the Elevator blogs and discussion groups on the internet.

Guy, aka, Pigpen was Harold's go-to repairman. He could do just about anything. Liners, valves, controller change-outs and you name it, Guy did it. I would sell a new controller and Harold would order up a new one from Delta. Guy would show up in his well-stocked van and "Bingo," it was a done deal and he was off to his next job. Like most of us in the business who have done this type of work, sooner or later a tragedy comes knocking. Guy's happened while he was doing a liner down south. He was on top of the car he had just secured in the overhead when the rigging failed. The car fell four floors. Luckily there was enough of the jack that they were removing to keep the car from hitting his Helper who was in the pit. Guy ended up with a broken back that kept him home for a year until he could return to work. The Helper walked away unscratched.

Jim was another Mechanic who worked with me. He was a good Mechanic with lots of experience. He came from Fresno and had owned his own company. He had lost his business and Harold picked him up. He had worked for Haughton and knew people with whom we had both worked. Jim got off on the wrong foot with Harold because he was using the Company's gas card to buy smokes and various other things. "Harold doesn't even smoke." Other problems started to crop up. I would get calls from the office asking me to go to a job because Jim had not been there for months. Harold was going to let him go and I convinced him to give Jim the San Jose State contract. It was a one-man route and you had to be there every day. Jim took that job and was able to finish up his elevator career and retire here in Monterey.

My immediate supervisor was Nancy. She had worked with Harold for years and more-or-less ran the Mechanics. She took care of payroll and billing. Some of the other guys had trouble with her, but I found out the best way to work with her was to give her, "No BS" ... just tell it like it is and there wouldn't be a problem. We worked very well together until the Company changed hands, and she lost her job. The best thing about working with Nancy was that she got things done.

Harold had a couple of repair guys who had been with him for years. The first was Bill, a steady, hardworking, accomplished Mechanic. He would call me when he got to town, let me know where he was working and that was it. The only time I saw him was when he needed keys or wanted some company for lunch or coffee. The other repairman was Jack. A big strong barrel-chested

Vietnam Vet. He did two tours with Americal. This gave us something in common. Harold gave him his toughest jobs. He would piss and moan to Harold about every little problem but he always got the job done.

For parts Harold had Larry. You know how it works, call the parts guy, tell him what you want and he gets it for you. I just wasn't getting my parts and it was starting to get serious. I didn't want to rat him out to Harold or Nancy, so I just kept trying until I figured out what was going on. For some reason, parts ordered in the morning showed up. Anything ordered in the afternoon never made it. From that point on I only ordered parts in the morning and everything was cool. It turned out the lack of attention in the afternoon was due to a six-brew lunch. See, if you try you can work around anything.

I settled in and started working on my route. It needed some work and after I got to all my accounts and got the starter contacts changed, it started running itself. Monterey is a small town and everybody knows everybody else. My service calls were more like social events. I had a great bunch of customers with a few exceptions. It didn't take long to separate the good from the not-so-good. My first encounter with a not-so-good customer was at a hotel on Cannery Row. This hotel was on my route list so I went over to perform routine service. I was exiting my van with my service bucket in hand when a huge Mercedes Benz zipped by and parked next to my van. It was big and very long; I think it took four minutes to drive by. The door swung open and out charged this little Asian lady screaming, "You touch nothing, I have own elevator man." I knew I had a problem here because I knew she owned other buildings on my route. She was really worked up so I said, "Okay," and gave her the keys to the machine room and headed for my next service. A couple of days later the office called and said I needed to call one of my customers. It was that same lady. "You come fix elevator." I checked my paperwork and found out all her buildings had OG contracts. Meaning just what it says, everything but inspection is billable. I went over to her building and found the car down, fixed it, don't remember the problem. I wanted to get off on the right foot with her so I just charged it off as routine service. A month went by and another call came in. "Junk in the door track." I billed her this time. The office called with another call on this same building. "You come fix elevator for free." My answer was, "no, no come fix elevator for free." "Okay, you come fix elevator; I pay but husband must watch." By now I could see this was going to be a very strained relationship. I hit the job and the husband watched. Problem, "husband have breath smell like vulture crotch." "I have other building, broken elevator, you go, husband ride with you." "No, husband no ride with me, against Company policy." Her old man tried to birddog me on everything I did. Even if I didn't have to, I left him standing all alone in the lobby, every chance I got. Years passed and when she finally figured out I wasn't out to bankrupt her, she settled down and became a pretty good customer. I had another OG over in PG and the whole family ran this hotel. Talk about cheap! They also thought we were gouging them on every call. One night a call came in that there had been a power failure and "Dad" was trapped in the elevator. I got up from dinner and made the ten-minute trip to get him out. I got there and one of the family members is standing at the front door . . . "We canceled." "I still need to check it." "No, we canceled." I was only going to charge them a half-hour anyway. Okay, no big deal so I went home and opened a Bud. Two weeks later I get a call from the same hotel. The maid had dropped the master keys in the pit. "When is my next service so we don't have to pay for the call? "I already did this month's service and I'm in Salinas. I'll be there in an hour." Which was really not true, I was right down the street. You know the rest of the story.

Monterey is a paradise and I was so lucky to be working here. What made it even better was Harold. He was the best boss I ever worked for. Nothing lasts forever and the majors had been courting Harold about a buyout. He finally caved in and I was now working for US and shortly thereafter, Dover. Dover then became Thyssen. My situation would change greatly.

The only good thing about this whole new deal was Jim. He had worked for US and Dover in the bay area. He was a Navy Veteran who had been a boiler man on an aircraft carrier during the

Vietnam War. His route was in Monterey and parts north. We now were working for the same Company. We hit it off immediately and became best buds. We had a blast working together. He was a very sharp Mechanic who carried a disorganized toolbox full of oddball tools from Harbor Freight. I mean like, who in the hell needs a 24/63 inch box end wrench? We became inseparable and we turned into a semi-pro comedy act according to our customers. I can't even count the times he made me laugh my ass off. One event in particular still stands out in my mind.

We had a new US job that was giving us a lot of headaches. Jim approached this troublesome job with his time-honored fix for about everything. Put Snubbers on it. Snubbers were actually capacitors he put on almost every job he did. He had a big freight in Salinas that had so many capacitors on it, I think it could have run for a day or two with the power off. Well anyway, back to our sick US Elevator. He installed his Snubbers expecting a miracle, and he saw one alright; he "Saw the Light." I was manning the disconnect, watching him work and noticed he had installed three of his "Fix-All's" on the main three-phase fuses in the controller. I had a feeling they shouldn't be there but maybe he knew something I didn't which happened all the time. "Don't look at it, power on," I replied and closed the disconnect. For a brief moment the machine room looked just like the bridge of the "Starship Enterprise" while under attack by the "Klingons." He didn't completely follow my instructions but the saving grace was that his eyes were closed during the explosion. His face looked like he had just pulled a twelve-hour shift in a West Virginia coal mine. Fortunately, the controller survived and didn't need a lot of help to be up and running again.

Thyssen was starting to wear me down. My route doubled overnight. My customers were asking, "Where have you been, haven't seen you for awhile." After twelve years working for Harold and more or less being on my own, the corporate control was getting hard to deal with.

I was servicing one of my jobs when one misstep ended my career. I took a fall on a car top and reinjured my back. I would need another surgery to repair the damage.

I had 40 years in the business and maybe this was a good time to just pack it in. That was 10 years ago and the best thing I ever did.

Work Safe!

VISIT THESE GREAT WEBSITES!

6462667R0

Made in the USA
Charleston, SC
27 October 2010